EVERY TWO MINUTES

*One Woman's Healing Journey
through Sexual Traumas*

ROSEMARY D. NEIDIG

ISBN: 978-1-4834-0178-2 (sc)
ISBN: 978-1-4834-0177-5 (e)

Library of Congress Control Number: 2013913286

Because of the dynamic nature of the Internet, any web addresses or
links contained in this book may have changed since publication and
may no longer be valid. The views expressed in this work are solely those
of the author and do not necessarily reflect the views of the publisher,
and the publisher hereby disclaims any responsibility for them.

Any people depicted in stock imagery provided by Thinkstock are
models, and such images are being used for illustrative purposes only.
Certain stock imagery © Thinkstock.

Lulu Publishing Services rev. date: 8/2/2013

Dedicated
To
Paul
Whose unwavering
Love and support
Sustained
Our relationship forever.

TABLE OF CONTENTS

FOREWORD

"Every Two Minutes" is an intimate journey into the life of a woman who has suffered and survived experiences that unbelievably all too many have had to endure at some point in their lifetime. The statistics say one in four, perhaps it is; maybe it is more. There were moments in reading Every Two Minutes that I related so deeply to the writer's search for peace and self-actualization and times when the writer's honesty provided me with hope for women and men to gain deeper appreciation for one another and an ever greater understanding and forgiveness for one's own self as well.

This is a story of crippling pain, devastating betrayal and tremendous loss but it is indeed a story of extraordinary triumph. The author's courage to share her experiences with her readers provides a platform for dialogue and a pathway to hope and healing for all who have the courage to stay with the story even when something in the telling breaks their heart or takes them back to a time that they do not wish to revisit.

Rosemary's story is validation for every woman who has either kept a "secret" or told someone and was not honored in their struggle for support and healing. It is required reading for every person who has either experienced sexual assault, lost part of their soul by some other life tragedy or for those who love, counsel or support someone who has been severely victimized and that is all of us. I honor Ms. Neidig for her openness, bravery and love.

Vanessa E. Hunter, M.H.S.
YWCA Social and Economic Empowerment Director

PREFACE

The commitment to pen my memoir began over twenty years ago. I had sought legal advice related to filing criminal charges against my perpetrator, only to discover that Pennsylvania Statute of Limitation had long expired. After my legal counsel knew the details of the criminal assault, he offered to appeal the state's statute through the many levels of the court system. I declined his generous offer because my recovery was in its early stages. I was too vulnerable to withstand public criticism that would likely be directed at me, my husband and children since this perpetrator was well known and held a respected position in the community. It was at that moment that I vowed to tell my story for all those assault victims who have lived through years of silence and lost legal options.

During the weeks and months of ongoing therapy, I maintained a personal journal. Those pages became the basis of my expanding awareness of the negative impact and unconscious influence of childhood and young adult attacks had on my beliefs, values and attitudes toward life. The comfortable coping skills that I had perfected over years, with expanded understanding, were actually out of control behaviors. The changes into a much healthier lifestyle is the power of my story. Those journals also became the starting place of this manuscript along with my revised perception of a lifetime of significant influences.

INTRODUCTION

As I begin to tell my story, I long for women and men to step out of the shadows into the bright light of self-realization, fulfillment and positive self- regard. This wish begins with me and extends to the women of the world. I tell my story to step into that light of healing. I ask you to take my hand and walk with me through my decades of darkness into light. If the journey has familiar scenes or conjures up distant places, bring yourself to continue your own journey. If this journey offers you a different perspective or a new insight, sharing my story has been more than worthwhile. Walk with me and with those in this world who also travel through the shadows into the light because "EVERY TWO MINUTES SOMEONE IN THE UNITED STATES IS SEXUALLY ASSAULTED"

PROLOGUE

Weekly counseling sessions with Caroll continued to unlock doors to childhood memories. Cradled in the soft leather folds of an overstuffed recliner, I narrated the good little girl's story. While the late afternoon light filtered through the overgrown house plants near our chairs in her office, it formed dancing shadow figures along the beige painted walls. Among the dark and light, an image of a young girl slowly emerged from the depths of my memory. She sat silently with her arms wrapped around her legs in the corner of my mind. She listened intently to stories of a happy child whose parents loved her. Her head dropped and she clutched her legs tighter as I told Caroll about wonderful Christmases at my grandparents' house in the quaint country village.

Were this child's memories different from the adult woman's who was seeking answers to a period of confusion surrounding the fatal car crash of her first husband in 1965, nearly twenty years earlier? This child's presence would significantly contribute to uncovering the truth of traumatic events that led to the illusion of a perfect, safe world instead of facing the crush of shooting pain and constant terror.

PART 1

CHAPTER 1

FAMILY BACKGROUND AND EARLY YEARS

November 6, 1942. "It's a girl!" When I took my first gulp of air, I am certain that my mother breathed a sigh of great relief. After suffering several miscarriages, she had at last succeeded in carrying a pregnancy to full term. But more importantly, she had delivered a daughter to her husband who was convinced that they were having a girl. I am certain that Mom must have been extremely unnerved for months after Dad's early pronouncement since Mom's life's mission was to please the man she had married. Her commitment to please was demonstrated often over the many eras with her.

I learned also that my dad was surrounded by men so it was no great mystery that he wanted a daughter. Born and raised on a farm, he and his three brothers were the vital links to survival for their parents. He knew only hard work from dawn until dusk, planting and harvesting the fields. In rural Central Pennsylvania, life was simply work, it eventually became his primary source of pride. Vacations were unheard of except for an occasional visit to a neighboring relative on Sunday when the Lord and my father rested.

Glimpses of my father's childhood were images of father and sons shoulder to shoulder behind the plow while their mother slaved over the kitchen stove cooking and canning. I was told that my grandfather gave Dad a strong work ethic; grandma gave him a strong body through hearty meals. That may have been the only way Mary Catherine knew to nurture her husband and sons. Dad's soul was fed by the small country Protestant Church where men studied the Bible together and sang hymns of praise to their Father God. Jesus was depicted dressed in white robes and carrying a lamb in a huge mural over the rural church altar.

When the Depression hit Dad's parents hard, he left the farm to work in the government sponsored Civil Conservation Corps (CCC). I have seen group pictures of a seventeen-year-old dad dressed in military uniform. He worked side by side with many other young men. They cleared forests, built roads through the Allegheny Mountains and sent their monthly allotments to struggling families. In 1939, when floodwaters threatened nearby towns, the CCC men were called out of the mountains to rescue the flood-ravaged valley townspeople.

Dad met Mom while he was sandbagging the Susquehanna riverbanks near her in South Williamsport. After a brief engagement and simple church wedding, my parents moved to New Jersey where Dad worked on a commercial farm until the newlyweds returned to mom's hometown.

Later, he spent from 1944 to 1945 in the Army during World War II working as an auto mechanic. Eventually he owned and operated a Texaco gas station in South Williamsport where he also repaired automobiles.

I do believe that Mom's life mission was to please the men who surrounded her. The two most important male images in her young life were an alcoholic father and God. She would tell stories that, as a youngster, she had a wonderful father but reality was too cruel for Mom. Her father's alcoholism brought with it an unstable financial life and rageful outbursts. Mom's reaction, I have learned, was not unlike those of other children of alcoholics who found themselves caught in the cycle of abuse. Her father drank, lost his job, drank *because* he lost his job, drank because he was not providing for his family, drank because his wife was the breadwinner instead of him, drank because his children had only the most meager of provisions and he drank until he exploded.

Mom eventually shared the true story of life with an alcoholic father. His rages were directed toward his wife, but as a teen, my mom often interceded and by doing so, became the target of his unleashed fury. Once when she stepped between her parents in conflict, her father's hurtful comment remained a painful memory for her. His raging response to her act was "Who do you think you are? God?".

Mom's sister was often angry too. She recounted a specific incident between them. Apparently my Aunt Rosemary pushed Mom around quite often. Their mother must have been frustrated by one aggressive daughter and the other daughter's passive reaction because she finally shouted, "Olive, hit her back!" Mom clearly remembered her mother's coaching at that moment. Mom said that she never was able to retaliate.

All she ever wanted was a happy father so she chose to remember the temporary calm after each alcoholic storm. The only way she could justify her father's fury was when she learned that her Almighty Heavenly Father raged too. Much later in life, she talked about the shame she felt watching her father stagger on the sidewalk toward her with his trousers saturated with urine. I was reminded of an occasion when I saw my dad's trouser fly zipper opened forgetting that he stood exposed outside our church waiting for Adult Sunday School to begin. I too felt that same shame. As a result of her teenage experiences, mom refused to ever put alcohol to her lips.

Mom believed the biblical story of Adam and Eve. She was Adam's rib placed on this earth to serve men. Later I realized that she vowed to do God's will and remain obedient to both her earthly and heavenly fathers. Mom's devotion to serve and Dad's work ethic were the foundation of their marriage and our family life together. He provided the financial stability that she desperately needed, while she provided everything that she thought her man needed.

Within a short period after their wedding, they bought a basic two-story frame house in a quiet neighborhood in North Central Pennsylvania. But W.W.II shattered all of our lives. The attack on Pearl Harbor in 1941 produced a dark cloud over the universe in which I was born. It blocked the sunlight of happiness and shadowed my household and neighborhood with fear and death. Later in my life with my mother, her stories about the war years suggested that although my parents willingly made the material sacrifices required by their government to support the war effort, they had difficulty with the emotional sacrifices.

Dad only spoke about his war experiences once much later. My parents had joined us in casual conversation around our kitchen table. The discussion was about our oldest son being drafted into the Vietnam War. Dad started to recount his WWII training experience for flight plane gunner. He and a buddy watched a plane full of trainees lift into the sky over the Texas Army Training Camp. As his story unfolded, Dad was gesturing by raising his arm to demonstrate the plane in flight. Then as I watched, his arm froze in midair; his voice vanished and his entire body was shaking. At that moment, it was evident that he had buried his fear of war experiences.

Mom could barely watch a plane fly overhead; her war memories haunted her for life. Also, until my father's death, mom gave a ten percent tithe to her church because she promised the financial commitment if God would bring Walter safely back from the war.

Within a year after my birth, Dad volunteered for military service. He had been exempt from active duty because of his employment in a local factory producing war aircraft but eventually he enlisted in the Army. Mom sought refuge in her neighborhood where she could be preoccupied with other women's lives and distractions to dispel her loneliness.

Sarah, the neighborhood matriarch, lived across the street from our home. There neighborhood women and children gathered around her kitchen table to help prepare meals for her large family while drinking warm coffee and filling Sarah's entire interior with chatter. Without a father and with a mother preoccupied with the war, I thought of Sarah as my second mom. Her home was alive and buzzing with activity while my home lay silent and cold.

Sarah was a soft, gentle woman. Her softness was her size, too. She was of medium build, with large soft breasts. She had a full figure clad in housedresses and aprons. When I hugged her, I felt her softness and warmth, unlike Mom's body that was always restricted with a girdle stiffness around her middle. Sarah's belly and chest were unrestrained. No false impressions and no make up; Sarah's only powder was flour smudged on her cheeks or nose from her daily kitchen chores. Sarah always found a few minutes away from her household demands whenever I crossed the street to her kitchen. Whether she was covered with flour from baking pies or engrossed in supper preparations for seven, she would put everything aside to offer a smile or a hug.

Although most of my memories are pleasant at Sarah's, I remember one confusing childhood incident in her home. On one of our daily visits across the street, I was placed in a wooden high chair and put in a narrow hallway between the kitchen and living room closed off by doors on each side, a punishment for my apparently bad behavior. I believe that Mom took a solemn oath never to rage at her child as her father had. Instead, when she felt angry, she separated herself from her child. As I sat there, too small to escape, I learned to be silent and to suppress my fear. A small window far above my head revealed a violent thunderstorm outside. The two sealed doorways on either side of the hallway shut off from the people I loved because I misbehaved. I cried but no one rescued the two-year-old from that dungeon. There I learned to submit to authority, my peace-loving mother. I learned that if I screamed during that lightning and thunder storm, no one would hear or respond. I wanted my daddy, my protector. To this very moment, thunder and lighting storms can bring ancient fear to rattle my calm mood, much like mom's WWII ghost-like planes.

While Dad was away, his mother became ill. Mom volunteered to care for Grandma when she was recuperating at her home. My grandparents had sold their farm earlier and lived in Rebersburg, a small country community surrounded by farmland in Central Pennsylvania. Their two-story frame in town reflected much about their farm lifestyle since it included a summer kitchen for the sole purpose of cooking and canning garden harvests. The huge living room with a bay window opened onto the main street; the large dining room and kitchen welcomed all for Grandma's special meals and the back porch led to gardens and sheds and a yard that stretched into farm cornfields. Upstairs, the four bedrooms and bathroom were adequate for this aging couple as well as visiting guests.

Mom was very eager to please her husband's parents, so she enthusiastically nursed my grandmother back to health while cooking and cleaning for the aged couple. My summer that year was filled with exploration and play. A metal washtub placed in their sunny backyard became my swimming pool. Whenever I wanted a break from the splashing cool waters, Grandpa took me into his garden to find the ripest red tomato and plucked it from the vine. His hearty laugh followed as I devoured the tomato instantly, ignoring the flood of juices trickling down my chin, neck and bathing suit. I felt very special that summer. I was his only granddaughter and his favorite. With Dad away, I clung to this man even tighter so I didn't miss Dad quite so much. Whenever mom needed groceries from Rebersburg's general store, the two of us went. We walked to the Rebersburg National Bank, the U.S. Post Office and the Protestant Reformed Church; all these places were on the one and only main street. I liked all the attention from grownups during those walks that summer. Grandpa even volunteered to help mom with my bath.

Several months later in 1945, mom and I went to Harrisburg to meet dad's military homecoming train. Uncle Paul, Dad's brother, chauffeured us to the train depot. A crowd of families were waiting to greet their returning soldiers. The moment I heard the whistle of the approaching train, my cheers instantly joined the chorus of greeters standing on the depot platform. According to mom, as soon as we were reunited, I curled up on dad's lap for the entire ride. She said that my remark, "I love my daddy," upset her because I had never told her that I loved her. Can jealousy exist between mother and daughter?

After Dad returned from his military service, the three of us were reunited. To the public, our family photo could have almost been on the cover of Good Housekeeping Magazine because Mom worked continuously to present a perfect portrait. Olive radiated a serene aura of devoted wife and mother. Her carefully selected wardrobe, makeup and hairstyle completed the illusion that was my mother. Her outside appearance was most important.

Walter's rough, oil stained hands were carefully concealed for the photo. Instead of his mechanic's uniform, he wore a pin striped suit, matching tie and dress shoes. If you looked closer though, you might notice a slight sparkle in his eye captured by the photographer. His somber mood was much more common for this working class head of household.

I took a position between my parents, wearing a Cinderella dress, patent leather Shirley Temple shoes and a lace petticoat purchased from last week's receipts at dad's gas station.

This portrait came to represent a clear message. Nothing was more important to mom and dad than presenting a perfect image. From then on, my conduct was measured against a magical little girl who danced around, taunting and teasing me into perfection.

I labored hard to mend and refine my behavior to gain my parents' approval. Usually I managed to determine those aspects of acceptable behavior to keep my world smiling back. Unspoken rules like "avoid conflict at all costs", "cleanliness is next to Godliness" and "silence is golden" were a few of the values that prevailed. Although articulated in so many words, my bedroom was void of clutter, conversation at the dinner table was unheard of, and playing in the mud after a Spring rain was forbidden. Mom's acceptance and love were solely dependent on my performance because parents who believed in perfection demanded a perfect child.

Occasionally, even my best efforts were inadequate to control myself and others. One particular "bad little girl" incident occurred when I had gotten into some childish mischief. I don't recall the crime; this was most likely the beginning of my repressed memories. It must have warranted capital punishment though because mom demanded that I select my own weapon. She usually swatted my buttocks with her hand or a flyswatter instead she insisted that I go to the backyard lilac bush, choose a strong branch and return to the dining room. My dilemma grew more and more intense as I trudged slowly toward the bush at the furthest corner of our backyard. From the black and white world of a child, I had two choices: walk very slowly to delay the inevitable stinging pain on my bare legs or hurry to end this crisis more quickly. My emotions were bubbling up inside, my heartbeat was pounding in my ears and I knew I was doomed.

Suddenly, I realized the ultimate cruelty of this punishment. While I was exploding with emotion, Mom stood calmly at the backdoor with no sign of being emotionally involved. Not Mom. She had discovered a clever way to avoid all of that and I was furious. I broke off a low hanging branch from the lilac bush, turned and marched toward the backdoor, determined to spoil her clever plan. I opened the door to face her stone cold eyes, with the fire of anger in my own. I handed her the switch. Then I ran past her into the dining room; my tiny legs had wings as I circled the drop leaf table just inches out of her reach. I succeeded! She was yelling and animated as we raced around the room. For a few brief moments, Mom and I were both emotionally involved in this act of conflict. Of course I still felt the sting of the lilac switch but I was elated. My fear had vanished that moment when I took control in my first act of defiance.

Another prominent figure in my childhood was Nana, mom's mother. I knew very little about her younger life but soon recognized her dignity and gentility. She was a talented seamstress, a woman's woman, who wholeheartedly welcomed my visits to her solitary life. She had told her husband to leave because of his drinking, and in reflection, she seemed at ease with her independence. Models of independent women were rare in my youth so Nana's world became an example I appreciated as an adult. Her unassuming nature allowed me to spend many hours in close companionship with her, free of the expectations and "good little girl" rules. Nana's peaceful nature calmed my own when we shared together.

I remember wanting to run away from home; I was about the age of five. I stuffed some underwear in my dolly's suitcase determined to walk to Nana's house about a mile away; most five-year-olds don't have much sense of distance. But before I could walk out the door, Dad, who seldom became involved in the conflicts between Mom and me, stepped in, pointing his finger in the direction of my bedroom until I "calmed down."

CHAPTER 2

SCHOOL DAYS

When I was old enough to move into the wider world of society, I enjoyed school and church because I realized that others smiled back. The lessons on gaining approval from mom and dad continued to serve well in this new, wider world. In elementary school, teachers reinforced my good-little-girl façade. My report cards reflected excellent grades and check marks of approval in the conduct column, gaining a respectable reputation as I made my way through the public school system. Classmates and I were a homogenous group. Born during the war, we all were in need of lasting bonding to dispel the cloud of confusion that overshadowed most of our infancy. Our common middle class values formed an ethic of competition and achievement. It appeared that most of us girls were striving to reach the elusive " good enough" plateau. I was not alone in my struggles. Numerous studies conclude that "gender awareness appears in children as early as two years old." "Elementary schoolchildren typically can verbalize many established gender rules, such as what behaviors are expected of girls and boys." (Judith Worell and Pamela Remer)

There was one unfortunate incident that marred my otherwise unblemished reputation. In fourth grade at Southern

Avenue School, I thought my image was secure in Miss Edward's classroom. Her stern demeanor generally relented at the sight of my smile. However, there was no relenting. My crime was talking during class. When I realized that my apology did not soften her scowl, I stiffened for the punishment but was not prepared for what happened next. She dragged my body to the front of the classroom in full view of my peers, retrieved a roll of masking tape from her desk drawer, tore off a long piece and slapped it across my face from ear to ear, sealing my lips. Flooded with shame and humiliation, I could barely glance toward my shocked classmates. Miss Edwards then banished me to the closet for the rest of the afternoon. In retrospect, the accumulation of cruel messages from the highchair to the classroom intended to silence my voice was devastating but NOT totally. I simply refused to completely submit to authority, even to the highest power in my life.

My religious indoctrination began early. Church services at Messiah Lutheran were weekly events for my Protestant parents, with their daughter in tow. The most important element of my religion became the Christian music. God, our Father, was an adult concept; invisible, much like my busy earthly father and a frightening creature who saw and knew everything that I did, said or thought. Only through music could God and I have a relationship. Somehow as I sang the church hymns, I was energized through my voice. Church songs spoke of love, justice and hope. I longed to believe in the goodness of others.

Music was also the best thing about Christmas Day too. For as long as I can remember Christmas morning, the living room was decorated with a small evergreen sparkling with tinsel, colorful balls and bright lights. Packages wrapped in red and green paper were under the tree. One Christmas when I was in elementary school, a completely furnished dollhouse was a Santa Claus surprise. No matter where I lived throughout my life that special gift went along. I have realized that this little house with its miniature furniture became the only place that I completely controlled.

Most holidays, a new doll was among my childhood presents. Soon after the final package was opened, my parents were packing our Chevy with more presents and mom's favorite baked goods ready for our trip to my grandparents in Rebersburg. I wanted to stay and play but instead was ushered into the car's backseat usually cuddling a new doll. I felt better when mom and dad started singing Christmas tunes from the instant we pulled away from our driveway until we reached dad's parents' home an hour and one half later. I still know the words to most Christmas Carols but repressed any feelings of anxiety.

In contrast to this confusing and uncomfortable church teachings, an endearing pastor, Reverend Raymond Shaheen, warmed my heart. He radiated a trustworthy kindness to all his congregation and especially for us children. I was fortunate to have him conduct instruction classes to prepare for my Confirmation Rite at thirteen. Those weekly classes under his guidance brought emotional balance to an otherwise difficult period in my early teens. Love, in its many forms, drew me like a magnet during those years.

Church services became another routine to maintain family harmony which I managed best by singing my way through the façade. But whenever I felt myself slipping into total submission, I would slip away from a Bible study class for a cherry coke at the nearby soda fountain with my friends.

The most intimate relationship I have had with music began when I was ten with the arrival of an upright player piano. I had begged my parents for a piano because I realized a growing passion for music. They agreed on the condition that I submitted to weekly piano lessons and daily practices. I promised to faithfully learn the music if only I could have a piano.

Her tall dark wood frame was a welcome sight as the movers lifted her in place in our living room. I did keep my promises, attending lessons and practices but sheet music of Rock and Roll songs and television's Hit Parade songs became my favorites.

As much as I loved my piano, I would have easily traded it in exchange for a sister. If I had a sister I would have shared so many things with her. I imagined the two of us lying across my bed laughing and talking for hours. I would have told her all my secrets and we teased each other about all kinds of silly things. I would have told her about the things that were scary. We would have had pillow fights and rolled around for hours. She would tell me how silly I was to be scared and would hold tight when I cried. She would get angry if anyone hurt me and promised to stay close by so nobody could hurt me again- a sister instead of a piano.

CHAPTER 3

PRETEEN

I was ten and Mom was gradually easing her reins of control. On weekends during the school year and summer, I was exploring on my bike. My friend Barb and I often ventured across the river bridge to different neighborhoods, city parks and the local YWCA. Braver and more adventurous, Barb usually led the way to these new and strange worlds. During the summer of 1953, Barb and I were two-wheeling across the Maynard Street Bridge to Williamsport, through poor shanty neighborhoods, shortcutting through Way's Garden Park on the corner of Fourth Street and Maynard, to the YWCA's Day Camp for girls. This big bite of freedom was exhilarating; my energy level soared and I vowed to breathe freely forever.

Barb and I were discovering boys, too. We giggled and blushed when boys whistled as we biked through the main streets. Occasionally we stopped to talk to the guys along the way but Mom still had strict limits on those bike excursions, especially summer camp trips, and I refused to risk being grounded. However, two years later, restrictions were further diminished and I was permitted to go to the roller skating rink near the YWCA on Saturday afternoons.

The only prerequisite to freedom was completing my routine morning household chores. The ritual of scrubbing, polishing and organizing was almost automatic by then. Occasionally, while I dusted my bedroom shelves, my collection of miniature dolls were a reminder of the "good little girl" who was gradually fading. As I mopped the floor, a life size ballerina sculpted in my bedroom's linoleum floor who was frozen in space also reminded me of the magical child who danced around in my mind as I learned to please the grownups in my childhood. She too had almost disappeared from view. Replacing them, a preteen was emerging who followed the rules from Sunday through Friday, but then flexed her independent muscles on Saturday afternoon. My body shape was changing too. Small, budding breasts, narrower waist and fuller hips all suggested my emerging femaleness.

Those weekly adventures to the local skating rink were the center of my newly discovered universe at the age of thirteen. The boys in that part of town were much different from my male classmates. Older and more streetwise, these guys were bolder. They were rough and exciting in their James Dean jeans and T-shirts.

Barb and I loved pulling on our skates and circling around that rink for hours. Lights from the suspended crystal ball everywhere, dancing on the walls and sparkling on the smooth wooden floor. The music floated deep inside until my body swayed to its rhythm and my legs synchronized with its beat. With each lap around the rink, I felt the surge of life rising higher and higher in my body as the rush of air touched my face and tossed the hair off my shoulders. Then I floated away. Barb, the other skaters, the walls, the polished floor all vanished as the dancing lights, swaying music and I soared far beyond the rink; I lived for those moments of ecstasy. Whenever my weekdays seemed too demanding or my nights too restless, I drifted into the magic of excitement and freedom of the rink.

CHAPTER 4

HIGH SCHOOL TALES

I noticed that my body was a problem in seventh grade gym class at South Williamsport High School. This foreign land called high school held many new experiences but gym class was the most awkward. When I stepped into the girls' locker room, I entered an area of cold, grey cinder block walls, grey cement floor, blinding naked fluorescent bulbs hanging from high ceilings, dark green metal lockers and cold, narrow benches. I briefly thought that this must be like prison as I rushed to meet the demands of the instructor barking out orders, "Get into that gym suit now! Be out on the gym floor immediately." She snapped her orders with the authority of a head warden. We all undressed quickly out of skirts, blouses and loafers and donned our shapeless, blue cotton suits and white sneakers while jamming clothing, books and purses into the nearby lockers as ordered.

When the class ended, my life took an agonizing turn of events. The warden's words were like icicles chilling the entire locker room space, "Before you leave this room, you must take a shower." I froze. As an only child, I was unprepared for sharing the same room with other naked girls but for a postage stamp-sized towel to cover my developing body. I had once been to summer camp with other girls but there I had changed clothes in a private cabin. Here, no privacy of a bedroom or even a separate locker at the YWCA's Summer Camp, nowhere to hide, nowhere to crawl away unnoticed.

As I forced myself to move, I glanced around to see what my classmates were doing. Somehow they seemed to have mastered the art of getting from uniform to bath towel without revealing anything from armpits to knees. I was a fast learner and quickly followed their lead; so far, so good. The individual shower stalls with ugly plastic curtains were heaven. I inhaled fully as the warm water splashed against my nakedness. But emerging from that brief heavenly moment, I was face-to-face with what seemed like hell. No artist was in sight who could demonstrate how to transform my dripping body into a dry, fully clothed one without revealing any private parts along the way. I frantically searched for any clue to deal with this latest dilemma but something else caught my eye. As I watched my classmates, I noticed bras. Everywhere girls were struggling and fumbling with bras. I wore a camisole; not a bra. I thought all seventh grade girls wore camisoles-fancy undershirts-but not bras! Yet there they were, a sea of bras; everyone was wearing a bra. How I ever got through the rest of that day, I'll never know. My mind was totally focused on one mission: destroy that camisole and buy a bra! I wore a bra to my second gym class.

Eighth grade year went easier and I was beginning to notice senior high boys. I discovered that older boys were exciting; football games, basketball games, wrestling matches and baseball games became foremost on my social calendar. The star athletes became my heroes. Their muscular bodies and universal celebrity were thrilling. Since hero worship was a common thread among eighth grade girls, I felt more accepted by my friends.

In ninth grade, it was evident that all the girls had fuller breasts than I. They wore tight sweaters to emphasize their round and swollen chests. In the 1950s, the fad for girls was wearing a body-hugging cardigan sweater backwards with a pearl choker or a starched white cotton collar at the neckline. When my classmates wore those sweaters, boys noticed and smiled at them. I was secretly jealous of them; I wanted boys to notice me too. I was particularly interested in getting a Senior boy's attention. Dave was a handsome, mysterious, blond, blue-eyed guy. He was different from the football heroes who had captured my attention in eighth grade. Dave was shy and quiet, even sad. He was appealing as I watched him standing on the fringes of the elite crowd, just out of reach of acceptance. However, he was too intent on his group to even notice my subtle attempts to get his attention. I would have to do something about my upper body.

Then I learned there was a solution. Falsies! Those beautiful, full, soft perfect foam-rubber shapes were right next to the bras and panties at Woolworth's Department Store downtown. They certainly would be the key to attracting my secret lover, Dave. I invested an entire week's allowance on those treasures and as I slipped them into place in my bra, I glowed. I was leveling the playing field, so to speak. Now I could stand outside with my girlfriends before classes in the morning, sweater bulging in all the right places and Dave would have to notice. Our eyes would meet and he would know instantly that I was the only girl for him.

It was a cool September morning. I chose my outfit carefully the night before-a grey and pink plaid pleated skirt, pink nylon cardigan, bobby socks and penny loafers. When the clock radio's alarm went off, I jumped into action. Part of the morning routine before school was automatic; scrub my face, brush my teeth, comb the overnight twisted curlers to smooth my shoulder length hair.

Then came the deliberate dressing to achieve my goal. My excitement grew while I pulled on fresh panties and bra, gently inserting the newly purchased falsies in place. With shaky fingers, I fastened skirt and sweater buttons, then turned to face the full length mirror. After satisfied with my reflection, I used faint pink lipstick, the final touch, before leaving my bedroom. The bedroom mirror confirmed that my sweater had just the right effect.

I squared my shoulders as I approached the crowd at the school's entrance. Walking as casually as I could to disguise my pounding heart, I headed toward the group of my classmates but focused intently on the huddle of Senior boys where Dave was standing. I positioned myself so that he couldn't miss noticing my profile that morning. Nothing else mattered; nothing, that is, until I finally heard a chorus of voices calling my name. "Rosemary! Rosemary! What are you doing?" My friends' voices jolted me out of my fantasy. I realized that everyone including Dave was staring. They all discovered my secret. My plan was destroyed. Instead of getting Prince Charming's attention, I was in the eye of a shameful tornado sweeping up and tearing me apart. The sound of laughter was everywhere. My best friends created a protective circle until the sound of the school bell signaled the start of classes. I slipped into the girls' lavatory and remove those stiff, pointy foam-rubber creatures that had betrayed me when I needed them the most.

Then there was Jeb, shy, quiet Jeb. From the moment in second grade when he promised to marry me, Jeb's love stayed constant. By fifth grade, he and I were "a couple", physically matched because of our brown hair, brown eyes, dark complexion and short stature. Our first kiss in the third grade coatroom's darkness among wool coats and winter boots was the beginning of many more sweet, tender kisses in that coatroom. But I got bored easily with us when my social life expanded. Teenage sock hop dances, away football games and summer swimming at Mountain Beach led to meeting other boys who didn't know Jeb and I were a couple. Even after my experiments with older boys and our separation for five long years, when I reached out to Jeb, he warmly and gently accepted my open arms. Although we still shared our daylight hours, we hadn't shared our nights. Eventually our steamy bodies touched and my sexuality had been unleashed in the arms of my childhood love. At 16, Jeb and I shared our nights.

Something very significant happened during a chemistry lab class. As Juniors, we had ordered our graduation rings and their arrival had generated a wave of excitement. Jeb and I were at opposite ends of the chemistry lab but were always aware of each other. That day, I felt his eyes on my back and turned to where he sat. His warmth and gentleness flooded my senses as he purposely walked the length of the room until he stood in front of me. Holding his shining new class ring in one hand, he tenderly lifted my left hand in his, slipped his ring on my finger and whispered loving promises of together forever. Our classmates broke into a spontaneous cheer. But just a few months later into my Senior year, I was pursuing boys from a rival high school and Jeb's tarnished ring lay in a far corner of my dresser. Jeb's devotion during our young life together was both precious and frightening. Before our sexual experiments, I felt playful but after those backseat nights, I realized that my fear pushed him away.

CHAPTER 5

STEPPING OUT

April 1960: high school graduation was fast approaching. My job as co-editor of our yearbook was completed and my future was determined by a scholarship award from Rider College where I planned to major in journalism. Then I met Fred.

For several weeks, my friends Nancy, Carol and I had been meeting several young men at a popular hangout in Memorial Park across town. One warm evening as we all sat around in a red leather booth, someone suggested a swim. The guy knew of a plush pool on a wealthy estate nearby. It was secluded, but more importantly, he told us that the owners were away on vacation. We all took his dare to go swimming there with him.

As the excitement built in the booth, several other guys joined the group. One of the newcomers was a tall, handsome blond in his early twenties who offered to drive a few of us to the pool; he knew the way. I could barely keep my eyes off this beautiful man so I eagerly accepted his offer. As I slid onto the front seat of his white Ford convertible, my heart was on fire. No male had ever been so attractive not even my first lover Jeb. This tall, mature man was different. He had joined us but remained distant; I was intrigued.

The warm April air rushed through my hair and pressed against my flushed cheeks as the convertible sped along the city streets toward our destination with this gorgeous chauffeur at the wheel. The suspense grew as we arrived at the darkened mansion on Ravine Road. Excitement ran rampant in my veins; this adventure was so foreign to anything I'd ever known in my upbringing. Mansions and private pools had always represented a lifestyle far beyond my grasp. Those images belonged to the wealthy, the elite; they were something of a dream. That night, this dream suddenly became accessible for a swift, stolen moment with an element of suspense; we were trespassing on private property of the wealthy.

As Fred maneuvered his convertible into a secluded spot just behind the other carload, I was nearly exploding with anticipation of our criminal action. Nancy's cautions echoed in my head but I was already climbing the chain link fence surrounding the swimming pool. Shimmering in the moonlight, the cool blue water seemed to beckon me closer. I loved to swim, to feel the sense of freedom, gliding through the weightlessness.

Everybody was shedding shirts, slacks, shoes and socks; so I followed their lead. I was determined to enjoy this magical moment, to impress Fred with my daredevil spirit. I could not hesitate; there was too much at stake. Fred's steel blue eyes were even more attractive as I stood at the pool's edge, clad only in bra and panties. I knew that he watched as I gently broke the water's surface; my body silhouetted by the underwater lighting. Starlight, open sky and friends nearby, I felt like a water goddess who had just emerged into her kingdom where she reigned supreme. In these brief moments of ecstasy, no danger existed in her realm.

Then someone noticed a neighbor's porch light flicker on. The spell was broken; we all rushed from the pool. As we hurried to dress and make our escape, Fred was by my side, helping to scale the fence and down the wooded hillside to where he was parked. Chilled by wet clothes and hair, I shivered visibly until Fred put his arm gently around my shoulder. That small gesture of affection revived the magic of that night and I again felt like a princess riding next to my tall handsome prince.

Fred and I spent almost every night in each other's arms; our romance grew more intense with each passionate embrace. While he worked, I finished high school. When I walked down the aisle on graduation for my diploma, the era of teenage carefree life ended as I dreamed of becoming Fred's wife. The college scholarship became meaningless; my only purpose was spending forever in the arms of my lover. One evening, shortly after graduation, Fred told my parents that we wanted to get married. At 17, I would need their consent. There was a long silence. Mom moved nervously in the white padded kitchen chair, glancing toward Dad. In moments of major decision making, she always deferred to him. Dad was a man of few words, rarely entering into long, thoughtful conversations. When he did speak that evening, I sensed that an extremely heavy weight rested on his shoulders. My parents' disappointment was evident and Dad insisted that I have some kind of professional training before we wed. I recognized that stalling tactic from some of my younger, more rebellious days.

For instance when I was 14, I was determined to leave town, get a job and live independently, all because I was sure I was in love! My town is the birthplace of Little League Baseball with annual summer World Series. Barb and I rode bikes to the games, more interested in the players than the play. A team from Morrisville, Pennsylvania won the tournament that year. Because dad's brother and his wife lived in the same town as the baseball champs, we were determined to move, get jobs and live in our own apartment to be close to our World Series Champs!

Dad's wisdom prevailed then. He insisted that I earn at least $500 before I could move away with my friend Barb. He even offered a job that summer working at his gas station. I pumped gas, washed windshields, scrubbed greasy storage shelves, learned basic bookkeeping of his business revenue and expenses. By the time I earned $200 I had lost interest in leaving.

I agreed to attend the Williamsport School of Commerce for six months to satisfy his demands. By then I would be eighteen and nothing would stand in our way; however, something happened that frightened us both before I finished business school.

During the summer of 1960, Fred and I spent many hours with our bodies passionately entwined. Whether we were in the backseat of his convertible or lying on a beach blanket under the summer sky, we were cautious about our lovemaking. Fred almost always made sure he wore protection. Lulled into a false sense of security, we were shocked to realize that I might be pregnant.

As soon as I suspected what was happening to my body, I sought proof. I had heard about a test that could determine an early pregnancy, but I needed a physician. In our small town where privacy was a premium, I chose a "has been" doctor whose office was on Riverside Drive. He had a poor reputation and few patients in South Williamsport. His office was dingy, his manner gruff, but I felt anonymous there and our possible secret safe. After many agonizing hours, my pregnancy was confirmed.

As I hung up the phone, the truth hit hard. I could barely think clearly as I dialed Fred's work number. I felt my dreams come crashing down as the shame of an unwed pregnancy flooded my mind. Lost and confused, I moved through the next few weeks in a daze as Fred and I contemplated our future. He was Catholic; I was Protestant. Our religious differences were slapping us both in the face. I am not sure what happened but suddenly during those frightening weeks, the fetus spontaneously aborted. As I watched the bloody clots wash down the toilet, I felt relief. Our dilemma was over and we had a second chance at happiness. Only years later did I realize the horror of aborting my child. But then, I was only rejoicing and thanking God for giving us back our dreams.

Afterwards, we agreed that we needed to avoid moments of passion as much as was humanly possible. We even decided that I should accept the employment offer in another city after completing business school. Lancaster was only two hours away and we needed the distance to protect our future.

My first real job was employment at Armstrong Cork Company. I was working for a real business; a prestigious company. The well known manufacturing firm gave my eighteen-year-old ego a boost of pride.

Fred and my plan for the future was that I would continue working in Lancaster and we would see each other on weekends but not until I got settled into my new job and was living independently at the local YWCA's rented room. The plan seemed logical, yet what eighteen-year-old functions on logic?

During the hours between sunrise and sunset, I enjoyed the excitement of a new job and my increased independence. But at night, I sat in the solitude and silence of my four walls reading Fred's daily love letters and longing for the warmth of his arms. Those letters are now grey with age, tied with red ribbon among my memories of six lonely weeks in 1961. Neither of us could stand to be apart; six weeks already seemed like an eternity. Finally one more love letter was all I could handle; I resigned my job, packed my belongings and drove back to town in a blinding snowstorm to reunite with my lover. That weekend, we told my parents that we would get married with or without their permission. Dad and Mom were heartbroken by my decision but agreed to provide a small wedding reception for us.

Before we could be married in the Catholic Church, I would have to convert to his religion since interfaith marriage was forbidden. Fred's parish priest provided a crash course in Catholicism. I was baptized, confirmed and made my first confession and communion, fully indoctrinated in the catholic faith and worthy to become Fred's bride. While most of the rituals were similar to my Lutheran upbringing, private confession was different from the open recitation during Lutheran Church Services. I fumbled my way through that first confession with nervous statements of sinful acts, the worst being sex before marriage. I was told to say two "Hail Mary's" and one "Our Father" prayer to clear away my sins.

His family warmly accepted me into their German circle from the beginning of our love affair. While I felt my own parents withdrawing their support during those weeks of wedding preparation, I was overjoyed with the acceptance of my new relatives. Our wedding plans were not those of a young girl's fantasies, complete with a flowing white-lace gown and princess crown. Our wedding was a celebration of our mutual love. Nothing more, nothing less.

CHAPTER 6

MARRIAGE

As I awoke that morning, April 22, 1961, the clanging of pots and pans in the kitchen; the sounds of preparation for our wedding reception to be held in my parents' dining room for a few invited relatives later. My "bridal gown", the new navy blue suit and white blouse, hung neatly on my bedroom door and my suitcase lay open on the floor with a beautiful white negligee softly folded on top in anticipation of a blissful wedding night. But inside, part of my heart was aching. Every girl's dream of walking down the church aisle on her father's arm to meet her groom at the altar was not to be mine. My parent's one punitive act for my Catholic wedding; Dad refused to escort me down the aisle of Saint Boniface Church. He explained that his membership in the local Masonic Organization prevented him from participating in a Catholic service. I tried to understand but was disappointed that he put his membership ahead of his daughter's important day. As I silently prepared for the happiest hour of my young life, my mind focused on the glorious sunshine outside my window. I busily arranged my white veiled hat, checked and double-checked my gloves and pearl white Bible adorned with dainty carnations and streaming white satin ribbons. Occupied with rehearsing and rehearsing my wedding vows, I focused on the positive aspects of the day, trying to ignore the heartache. I refused to let their attitude spoil our wedding. When I finally sat before the vanity mirror, quiet but for the busy clinking of china and crystal downstairs, I voiced those melodious words that would define my new life: Mrs. Frederick Fischer.

Our wedding and reception were witnessed by relatives and friends. My Catholic instructor took his place at the altar. Fred stood in front of the altar, waiting my approach as the organist signaled my first step into the sanctuary. I heard someone whisper "good luck" as I inhaled deeply to calm the wedding nerves. All eyes turned to see my entrance. I vaguely noticed their smiles, the flowers on the altar and the sunlit stained glass windows as I slowly and deliberately moved toward the man who pledged his everlasting love. Once I reached his side, the rest of our wedding began to blur through my misty eyes, clouded by the overwhelming joy of this love bond. The only words that still echo from that moment were "I now pronounce you man and wife". I was truly and finally Mrs. Fred Fischer.

Nothing in life had prepared me for what followed. We moved, or more precisely, I moved into Fred's homestead. His father had died earlier. Mom Fischer relished our company and we could save money for that white picket fenced house, our American Dream. The three of us worked but night was difficult. Our privacy and our lovemaking were both compromised even though Mom usually fell asleep before ten o'clock. Whenever I complained about our living arrangement, Fred promised that we would move when I got pregnant. I was expecting our first child by November that first year and by March, we moved into a private rented bungalow on the outskirts of town.

My life as Mrs. Fred Fischer gradually became just that- one of having my life defined by him. Though I was employed and earning the larger income, Fred insisted that my paychecks went directly into a savings account for our dream home. Now it seems ironic somehow because I was an accountant for a national loan company by day and personally had no decisions in finances by night.

However, I loved the cooking, cleaning, washing, ironing, all the wonderful ways of showing my husband and our families that I was a competent woman at eighteen. My sewing projects on a used Singer machine were also designed to prove my adulthood to others, especially mom and nana, the professional seamstress. Before Easter 1962, I fashioned a spring maternity outfit. A dark pink skirt and full over blouse with soft pastel collar and cuffs was finished for Easter Morning Mass. When I got up that morning, snow covered everything outside our cottage. Instead of showing off my new fashion, I had to cover it with a winter coat. No chance to parade through the church with my proud creation, a missed opportunity to watch smiling faces and approving nods that I sorely needed to validate my adulthood.

Fred rarely complimented my wifely efforts and our friends seemed to lose interest in visiting our little house in the country. I was beginning to feel isolated in the evenings. My husband often disappeared after dinner. I soon realized that he was meeting his buddies at a tavern in town. Instead of confronting him, I spent lonely evenings housecleaning every cottage room to please the man I married. So as the birth of our first child neared, I busied myself with decorating the nursery and distancing myself from the increasing pain of our marriage.

My parents were not only attentive with their Sunday evening visits throughout our marriage but dad took care of our car from annual inspections, routine maintenance and filled our Ford's gas tank often. Neither mom or dad's support was done with great fanfare. I had come to expect their financial generosity.

When Fred and I moved into our first place and I was eager to have my piano, dad realized the upright player piano would not fit through the cottage's narrow doorways. Without further discussion, the next week a beautiful spinet piano was delivered to our living room.

CHAPTER 7

MOTHERHOOD

oug's birth was a joyful event. His tiny infant needs were new to me but I rejoiced in loving him. Fred's pride in his son restored his attention to his family and our renewed intimacy seemed to energize his whole being. His regular visits to a local bar ceased after Doug's birth. Instead, playful evenings of laughter echoed through our bungalow as we reveled in the ever new antics of our tiny, smiling infant son. I resumed household chores with enthusiasm as my happiness for child and husband became central to my life. When Doug was three months old, I returned to work, remembering our goal of owning our American Dream. My position as an accountant for a local General Motors finance office was rewarding, not only because of an adequate salary but adult conversations, special events when the latest car models were unveiled at dealerships and the responsibility that my position carried. I was contributing to the success of the financial office's results.

Balancing employment and household chores during the work week was a gradual learned skill. Mom's "work before pleasure" philosophy guided my management but more important was my desire to give Doug and Fred as much of me as possible. A sister-in-law's aunt eased the burden. She babysat for our son and later our daughter. Before she left each day, she prepared wonderful evening meals for our family.

Within two years of Doug's birth, I was pregnant again. We agreed that this was the season to find that dream home before our second child arrived. Several months later, we were standing in the middle of a bare kitchen in a small ranch in a suburb of Williamsport. Fred seemed ten feet tall as he held his son in one arm and drew me close with the other, declaring that this was our new home. We both beamed with pride, as arm in arm, we walked into each room, imagining the layout as we went.

Our daughter was born in the quiet stillness of an early morning dawn in April, 1964. After her birth, Fred became more domineering, insisting on perfection in my housekeeping. He also dominated our lovemaking; I was frightened and confused. His sexual demands had increased to nightly intercourse, even into the last month of my pregnancy. That last month, my excitement for our new baby was shattered by his unceasing sexual demands. When labor pains started early one evening, I silently thanked my unborn for one night without fear. While pacing the kitchen floor that night, it was my mother who counted my contractions while Fred slept unconcerned. Eventually, the intensity of labor forced him out of his sleep and into responding to the urgency. Our daughter entered only minutes after we arrived at Divine Providence Hospital's delivery room. Lorraine, her tiny body still coated in fluid, emerged from the darkness of my womb into the brightness and warmth of her new world. Our daughter's first cry sounded like one of protest. An omen, perhaps.

Here we were the perfect American family. Husband and wife with first born son and new daughter settled into our perfect white picket fenced prefab in Loyalsock Township complete with dog and backyard swing set. Fred even told an elderly neighbor that his life was complete. I returned to work shortly after Lorraine's birth, comfortable with the knowledge that our children were in the care of a competent babysitter. Fred's drinking subsided again as he refocused his energy. His obsessive sexual demands lessened with his reduced alcohol consumption which alleviated my fears. Only in reflection of Fred's behavior do I understand that his lineage of alcoholism plagued his own young adult life. But then I was content with our life together. I finally felt fulfillment in my role as Mrs. Fred Fischer, even though employment and parenting were very demanding.

He arrived in late afternoon when both children were napping. We sat at the kitchen table talking about Fred's death and I poured out my heart and grief, relating how difficult it was without some resolution to my questions about this unexpected tragedy. His responses about God's plan for our lives fell on my deaf ears. Feeling frustrated and disappointed, I decided to make coffee. As I filled the pot with water at the kitchen sink, my tears seemed to flow just as fast as the water running through the coffee pot. At least my back was toward Father; he couldn't see my flood of emotions. No need to have him know how frustrated I felt. That was until I heard his footsteps. Suddenly, the weight of a coffee pot overflowing with water hurt my arm but the rest of my body went numb. It must have been another one of those recent bad dreams.

CHAPTER 9

GENTLE SOUL

Little by little, my friends encouraged my reentry into the land of the living. They insisted that I spend Saturday nights with them, dancing and laughing. Their theory: no twenty-two-year-old woman is expected to be the sorrowful widow on the hill. Some of them even formed a monthly card club to provide me with another activity, another commitment, all in an effort to lift my depression. Nancy even convinced me to join her social sorority. She was relentless in pursuing my involvement in life.

One evening she announced her arrangement of a blind date. Her boyfriend's buddy had just returned from basic training with the National Guards. She planned for the four of us to go for dinner. I was less than enthusiastic, but Nancy, who so lovingly gave of her time for my well-being, insisted and I did not want to disappoint her.

Paul Neidig was certainly handsome in his military uniform. He was tall and lean. As I assessed this man across the table and heard his gentle voice, I felt the warmth of his soft eyes and appreciated his calm manner. I began to relax after a few hours of lighthearted conversation and after-dinner drinks. At the end of the evening, he reached for my hand, held it gently in his own just briefly and said good night. As I looked up to meet his eyes, a wave of warmth touched my heart. A safe feeling that I barely recognized but I did sense something very different about this pleasant stranger.

Over the next few months while we dated, our relationship continued to intensify, spending most evenings together getting better acquainted. I watched Paul playing with Doug and Lorraine. Sensitive to their loneliness, he devoted early evenings entertaining them. Once they were safely tucked into bed, we talked, touched and laughed together into the early mornings. One of our romantic "dates" was hamburgers by candle light on a card table in my living room, a fond memory of our early dates together.

Fred had been killed in February of that year and my grieving had been replaced by this man's gentleness and safety in six short months. Our lovemaking had become spontaneous and somewhat careless during that period until I discovered that I was pregnant. My heart sank because I was certain that Paul was not ready to assume the roles of husband and father. I had already decided to have this baby alone and was hesitant to broach the subject at all with him. But Paul noticed my withdrawal and insisted on an explanation, so I reluctantly disclosed the news of my pregnancy and my plan. I saw anger in his gentle eyes as he confronted me. He said I was denying him any opinion about this decision and this baby was his, too. I could feel his deep hurt and disappointment in my independent handling of the situation. That night, after hours of tears and uncertainty, I pushed away any doubts and collapsed in his arms.

We were married on October 16, 1965, surrounded by loved ones, well wishers and two very young children. In sharp contrast to my first wedding, I designed every detail of the celebration to reflect the present and the future. The only reminder of the past was the peach-hued gown that I selected for our wedding. White symbolized the mantle of purity and virginity, none of which was appropriate.

The church pews were filled with those people in my life who mourned my loss in February, now rejoiced with us in October. Doug and Lorraine, our most precious guests, enjoyed the celebration in toddler fashion, captivating the hearts of all present as they danced in the arms of Mommy and their new Daddy at our reception. Paul truly loved them as his own.

He was eager to adopt them, so on Valentine's Day the following year, the four of us were sitting in Judge Greevy's chambers for the adoption proceeding. Nearly fifty years later, I stepped again into that same judge's chambers. This time I was interviewing the first female judge who occupied that office. As I gathered information for an assigned newspaper article, I glanced to the two leather seats that faced the expansive wooden desk and remembered Paul seated on one chair with Doug on his knee; I sat on the other, holding Lorraine on my lap while the president judge signed the official papers for Paul to legally adopt the children, whom he had already loved. For a brief moment that 1966 memory brought tears.

Within one year of Fred's death, life was mended. His children were lovingly transferred into the arms of a new father and our union was complete. I was living as if yesterday never existed. From the young girl's first love with Jeb to the young woman full of excitement at her first wedding to a young mother overjoyed with love for her children to the tragic death of Fred and the young widow's pain eventually transformed into the peace of remarriage and a restored sense of hope.

CHAPTER 10

GROWING FAMILY

Paul Jr. arrived in May of 1966, happily greeted by his brother and sister, grandparents and his extended clan. I soon realized Paul's strong affection for children had been rooted in his loving mother and responsible father who willingly sacrificed their own desires to respond to their children's needs. Although there was limited financial resources, there was a firm bonding between parents and adult children. Paul and his siblings still remained closely connected to their parents who enjoyed each new grandchild, welcoming each into the ever widening circle of love. Most of Paul's brothers and sisters were married with children and lived nearby. His mother continued to nurture her family by preparing feasts to follow weekly church services. All were expected to pay homage by partaking of this family meal each week. If anyone was absent, Mom worried until she received an explanation from the absentees. Even then, her disappointment was evident until the absentees were taking their rightful place at the dining room table. Those weekly family gatherings filled a void in my life as I absorbed the warmth and affection as a part of this large family. Finally I had the sisters and brothers that I had longed for when I was growing up alone. My parents were also faithful grandparents, spending nearly every Sunday evening visiting their grandchildren. This tradition was welcomed by us all.

Much of my energy during the first years of our marriage was focused on our three small children, our relationship and Paul's family. I had not returned to my job after Lorraine was born. Our finances provided the chance to be a stay-at-home mom for awhile. I enjoyed afternoon coffee klatches with several sisters-in-law while our children had built-in playmates in their many cousins. Paul's brother Dave and his wife Elaine became our close companions. The two brothers enjoyed organized softball games together, the four of us joined an evening bowling league and our weekend entertainment usually included relaxing at a local bar with Elaine and Dave. Elaine and I were nearly the same age; we seemed to be able to talk for hours about virtually everything and enjoy every minute of our friendship. Spending afternoons in Elaine's kitchen often reminded me of Sarah's kitchen. We laughed, cried and talked for hours together.

Greg, our fourth child, was born a few months after Paul Jr.'s second birthday in 1968. He received the same hearty welcome as each of our children. When he was born, the attending physician cautioned about having more children. Some physical complications during pregnancy had signaled risks to future pregnancies but I listened only halfheartedly and without personal concern. I was much too excited about our newborn's care to be distracted by technical medical jargon. My world was perfect.

In typical Donna Reed style from television fame, life revolved around family and home. I attended to their physical needs with a daily routine of cooking, cleaning, laundry, sweeping, dusting, polishing, sewing, shopping and orchestrating the activities of four small children. I even managed to volunteer for neighborhood fundraising events and supervise the recesses at their parochial elementary school playground. From morning to night, life offered constant opportunities to reinforce my Perfect Wife and Mother roles. I was truly blessed. God may have taken away my first husband but now He was generously showering us with unending blessings and I was grateful.

CHAPTER 11

FRESH AIR

S o grateful for blessings that when I read an article about the Fresh Air Fund, I was intrigued. The summer program linked New York City children with others in rural areas outside the metropolitan area. Bringing children from the hot asphalt to a vacation in a much different environment appealed to me. I thought *"what a wonderful opportunity for our family to share our good fortune."* What I didn't anticipate was the gift of two beautiful children who taught so much.

The first summer, William entered our lives for two weeks. From the minute I watched him step off the Lakes to Sea Bus, this wide eyed, five- year-old captured my heart. It was his excitement when he spotted a squirrel, his amazement when he learned that we lived in the upstairs TOO and his worry that sharks swam in our backyard pool. I marveled at his unceasing curiosity. In two short weeks, we introduced William to picnics, fishing and rides in the countryside for spotting deer. And I was certain that William would be invited to return the following summer.

The next summer, 1969, I eagerly anticipated William's visit. That morning when a phone call came notifying me that William had missed the bus, our children's excitement turned into quiet sadness. I tried to explain the situation even though

CHAPTER 12

AND BABY MAKES FIVE

My Catholic faith strengthened as we attended Mass regularly, observed every day of obligation and practiced all the church's mandates. Our children were enrolled in parochial school and attended mass with us as soon as they could sit quietly. Church services became opportunities to thank God for His many blessings. Each Sunday as I knelt silently in prayer my eyes filled with tears, tears of joy or so I thought. I often cried silently when watching a sad movie or whenever I received a special token of affection from Paul. My tears were an expression of feelings that I did not always understand but accepted as a welcome release of emotion.

It had been four years since our last child was born so I was overjoyed when I became pregnant. Even though the gynecologist repeated his concerns, my joy outweighed any fear. I refused to allow anyone to interfere with my "everything-is-fine" attitude.

Everything *WAS* fine until the seventh month of this pregnancy. I had spent the day canning tomatoes from our garden. After four hours of cleaning vegetables and sterilizing and filling crystal-clear jars with steaming red tomatoes, I was finally submerging the last of the jars into the boiling water on the stove. The heat from the stove and the hot September afternoon sun permeated my skin. Perspiration flowed freely down my face, arms, and legs. I barely noticed the twinge of pain from my swollen womb but as I stepped away from the stove, a small pool of red fluid caught my eye. Just then, another jolt, now stronger, more painful, cramped my body. Hours later in Dr. Hipple's office, I learned the protective fluid surrounding our unborn child had burst. I was strictly ordered to curtail all unnecessary activity, avoid all lifting and elevate my feet as much as possible. With four children and a personal penchant for perfection, I stupidly continued to manage my household on my own terms, essentially unrestricted. I ignored most of my physician's cautions until I became sluggish and feverish. Infection had taken hold and our baby and I were both in danger.

Paul frantically drove to Divine Providence Hospital. After a battery of x-rays confirmed their suspicions, a team of surgeons recommended delivery by caesarian section. They somberly prepared us for the possibility that our daughter might not survive the delivery because of infection and premature development. They also recommended immediate delivery to avoid increased risk to both of us. After my water broke six weeks early, my fragile daughter had sought protection in the uppermost part of my uterus but now infection was threatening her existence. True to my positive attitude in any situation, I assured the medical team that she and I would be "fine".

As the doctors released our new daughter from her uninhabitable abode of seven and a half months and placed her directly into a sterile incubator, my heart immediately filled with love for this tiny survivor. The surgeons were directing their attention to complete the procedure. Meanwhile, I heard voices saying to Paul that a hysterectomy was necessary. The Catholic hospital administrators were advised of the necessity for surgery and Paul and I agreed that our family was complete; we both accepted the reality of the hysterectomy. Besides, we now had five beautiful, healthy children.

Valerie's first two weeks of life proved her incredible will to survive. Her weight was the center of every nursery attendant's concern. With their constant nurturing and attention, her birth weight steadily climbed to the requisite five pounds without so much as an ounce drop. For one agonizing week, I watched her being nurtured by one white coat angel after another in her isolette, while I stood behind a glass barrier, aching to hold her in my arms. The moment finally arrived for the mother-daughter reunion and my painful longing dissolved as she rested her tiny head next to my heart and slept peacefully for hours nestled in the circle of my arms.

This was a rewarding and fulfilling period; the renewed joy of motherhood outweighed the many demands of childrearing. Each small accomplishment, every moment of childlike wonderment filled my days and weeks with contentment. Pictures of Easter egg hunts, Christmas morning chaos and picnics flash by as I remember this precious interim in our life. But as the financial demands increased and managing an inflated 1970s budget became more and more of a challenge, I realized that I would soon need to rejoin the workforce.

CHAPTER 13

REENTRY

There I stood at a crossroads. With a twelve-year-old high school diploma and a brief work history just as old, I knew my employment chances were slim. I turned instead toward community college business courses. Dad's voice of encouragement for education echoed in my mind.

Since I had been away from the job market for well over a decade, I decided to upgrade my skills first. The staff at Williamsport Area Community College were confident that I could attain an associate degree in business with evening classes which would allow for both student and mother roles. The timing seemed perfect. Valerie would be entering kindergarten when I was graduating from college.

For three years, I attended evening and weekend lectures, studied afternoons next to the three older children while Paul entertained the two younger ones. Our household fell into a routine around my college course schedule. I honed my management skills even finer than before. I put laundry and meal preparation together, running from kitchen to basement at the buzzer's signal of the dryer or washer. I used the crockpot for slow cooking, microwave for hurry-up meals and dishwasher to eliminate wasted minutes at the sink. All the kitchen appliances were called into "active duty" during my college semesters. Our sons and daughters also were enlisted for basic household chores.

The final year of my course study required attendance at regularly scheduled classes but by then the college was providing childcare services for parent-students; so mother and daughter attended college together that last year.

Graduation 1977: a day of personal pride. Walking up to receive my degree and an award for a perfect 4.0 average was a boost to my self worth. This degree and those perfect grades validated my individual identity. Until then I had taken pride in nurturing others but this accomplishment was mine alone.

I had been employed for several months before graduation. My clerk's job at the Lycoming County Court Office for child support was my first re-entry into professional life. My Associate Accounting Degree was the basis for managing a multitude of financial activities in the small office. Under the watchful eye of Esther, the only other woman in the five person office, I learned the details of the child support program. Three male court officers managed the growing caseload of separated and divorced clients with children. Just before my graduation, one of the officers resigned. I was encouraged to apply for the position since the court system had a policy of hiring within the organization whenever possible. The combination of Affirmative Action Laws that were sweeping the country and an organized campaign for a female officer by a group of local women contributed to the President Judge's decision. Graduation was Sunday and Monday morning I sat proudly behind the desk as the first female child support officer in Lycoming County Court System's history. I experienced some resistance from older male attorneys specializing in child support and custody laws but generally the entrance of a woman into the male dominated legal arena was unremarkable.

CHAPTER 14

SUPERWOMAN

Over the next few years, I continued to pursue my professional career while maintaining a strong commitment to our growing family. Twenty-four hours were never long enough to perform all these roles to perfection: juggling eight hour work, meals, laundry, PTA, high school sporting events, kids' studies and school projects. I was racing around from dawn until dusk to mirror the 1980s Supermom who was depicted as having a briefcase in one hand and a child in the other. We women were told that we could have it all.

Paul reluctantly stood by my side, offering support whenever I slowed down long enough to reach out to him. His frustration was evident; he was disappointed with the lack of intimacy between us but understood the financial need for a second paycheck. Assuring him that I wanted to be the very best wife, I begged him to be patient. I suggested that the children were getting older and their demands would lessen. Two in high school, one in junior high and two in elementary school, these babies were spreading their wings and soon would be leaving the nest.

We parents, like most, made the best of each moment, dealing with the challenges as they arrived. Vacations were escapes that we could step away from the everyday demands and enjoy the freedom of getaways together. From the beginning of our marriage, summer vacations were camping trips. Usually we spent a week along the Atlantic Ocean in Delaware in a tent camper. For a mere three dollar daily rental fee in a state campground, we had the luxury of beachfront accommodations and hours of surf and sand within a short walk. We had happy playful children building sand castles and dancing at the water's edge. Those yearly trips inspired us to dream of an extended cross country excursion. After lengthly discussions about such an adventure, Paul and I decided to make our dream a reality since our oldest would be entering his senior year at South Williamsport School District in the Fall of 1979.

Months of pouring over travel brochures, negotiating with employers for extended vacation, locating a rental recreational vehicle, listing supplies and wardrobe needs for eight and arranging for Lydia to join us, we set out to see this country. Having promised ourselves and the children that we would show them the natural beauty of their land, we finally launched our adventure: The St. Louis Arch, the cornfields of the Midwest , the Colorado Rockies, the breathtaking Grand Canyon, Arizona Desert, and California's Pacific Ocean. We toured national parks, San Francisco, Los Angeles, then headed for Utah. This 7,000 mile journey held different memorable moments for each of us but landmarks like Mt. Rushmore and Yellowstone National Park remain vivid. I now attribute this trip as a symbol of the celebration of our family unit and marked the end of an era. For one glorious month, our life was ideal as if afloat in an invisible bubble of happiness.

In the midst of the ongoing changes at home, I was also experiencing changes in the office. The new President Judge Raup insisted on more aggressive child support enforcement; my supervisor resisted. The changes were too difficult for the supervisor to accept and he agreed to relinquish his position . I vied with my co-workers for the administrator's position but was shocked when I was selected to direct the Domestic Relations Office. The role as director became the focus of my professional life as I strived to meet and exceed the expectations of the court administrator. Complicated Federal and State government regulations and complex court case law were no match for my determination to prove myself as the first female administrator in the local court system. The development of more aggressive court procedures to address deficits in child support orders, implementation of a computer system to enhance enforcement and management of a growing staff of professionals filled my business roles. Then two catastrophes hit simultaneously and the next several months were a nightmare.

The Spring of 1980, Lorraine was restless. Our older daughter's continued defiance grew increasingly stressful on all of us. One night, long after her curfew, we found her lying in the back yard. Paul's and Lorraine's tempers crashed into each other. Before either one did anything that could cause physical harm, I told her that we could no longer tolerate her behavior and she would have to leave. But when our 16-year-old stormed out of the house, I knew my hasty reaction had just fed her defiance. Paul and I held each other in silent grief that night as well as the next seven long, agonizing days that followed.

At last, the phone rang. Her voice was the sweetest sound I had heard for what seemed like an eternity. After several moments of disbelief and euphoria, I swallowed the lumps in my throat, gasped for air, fought back the sea of tears filling my eyes and found my voice. I heard myself calmly telling her that we missed her. Paul and I had agreed that we would not interrogate her, so I simply asked if she was all right, trying to keep my voice from quivering. She was in the Midwest headed for Omaha where her boyfriend lived. We arranged to send her money and a bus ticket so she could travel safely to her destination. As we talked that night, my arms ached to hold her close and keep her safe from limitless dangers. Instead, I had to trust a faceless bus driver to transport her to Omaha. She reached her boyfriend's place safely and his parents graciously received her into their home. Many years later she was able to talk about her cross country trip when she was fortunate enough to hitch rides with fatherly truck drivers.

This personal crisis erupted in the midst of a professional hurricane that swept through the entire child support department. The position that I held was less than a year old when the county's District Attorney requested a private meeting.

CHAPTER 15

CRISIS

The District Attorney started the meeting with this remark, "I have received a criminal complaint about one of your enforcement officers." I chuckled to myself. Clients paying child support were always complaining about having to pay "too much" and custodial parents never receiving "enough" child support payments. I asked the D.A. for details of the complaint. He explained that on several occasions over the past few months this particular officer had called the complainant and requested child support payments in cash. This public servant supposedly threatened to use his position as a court officer if the man refused. The individual met him, paid the cash, then immediately contacted the district attorney's office. I simply refused to believe the allegations; I agreed, however, to meet the D.A. after hours.

After the court house staff left at 5:00 p.m. and the office lights were dimmed, the district attorney and I met behind locked doors. Only after several late night reviews of the records could I accept the fact that this trusted employee had cleverly manipulated the payment information on the computer and covered his crime. For the next three weeks, I maintained a normal 9-to-5 routine in the office, then spent evenings searching case files for similar patterns of deceit while the D.A. prepared the victimized client for the next contact. With marked cash and a hidden tape recorder, the evidence for a criminal arrest was secured. A sheriff's deputy arrested and arraigned the criminal meanwhile I quickly informed the office staff before television cameras and reporters invaded our front door. In rural Pennsylvania, crime by a public official made front page headlines and TV news for weeks following the arrest.

Shock waves rocked the entire staff and unrealistic mistrust of all court officials spread throughout the community. Special auditors acted quickly to determine the extent of criminal activity through interviews and case file analysis. When the dust settled and the roller coaster activity slowed, the officer's history of theft and deceit documented his extensive abuse of power. Unfortunately his trial and sentencing only fueled the outrage which already stung my staff and clients alike.

A Philadelphia judge had been appointed to insure impartiality. But after hearing the case, he compared white-collar crime to cheating on income tax forms, completely ignoring the violation of public trust that court officers are expected to adhere to. The judge's sentence of probation stunned everyone including the district attorney who prosecuted the case. For months afterwards, the department staff was repeatedly accused of stealing child support monies. "After all," clients said "If one of you could steal, what was preventing all of you from doing the same thing?" Each incidence, my guts silently raged as I calmly reassured the person that the criminal had been convicted and we could be trusted with their child support money.

Scattered throughout this chaotic period, one bright spot emerged. Across the state, other child support agency directors extended words of encouragement and confidence in my ability to weather the storm of public criticism. This rare experience of dealing with criminal acts within the department afforded me an "expert" status among my colleagues. At the next Pennsylvania State Association Conference, I was asked to address the members on the subject of fiscal safeguards for child support funds. Public speaking had been frightening but I was so angry after months of constant turmoil that fear had no place as I stepped up to the microphone and hot television lights to alert colleagues of the potential dangers inherent in the fiscal management. Shortly after my presentation, I was elected to the state association's board of directors where my career took an entirely new turn.

My Supermom image continued to provide a façade to deal with the loss of children and the management of an ever growing staff at work, repeatedly achieving record breaking child support collections. But as a wife, I was still keeping my marriage partner at bay.

It was 1980, Doug graduated from high school, chose a career in auto mechanics and fell in love and married Vicki, all within a span of two years. Two other important milestones occurred within that period because I also became a grandmother at age thirty nine in 1981.

Lorraine had remained in Omaha after her rebellion at sixteen. She and Bob lived with his family until they were able to afford their own apartment. Shortly after they moved, their son Joshua was born.

CHAPTER 16

LIVES OF TEENS

From 1980 to 1985, our son Paul's development took some major twists and turns. When he was a toddler and slipped into the five foot depth of our backyard pool, he was a water baby. By age twelve, he was taking adult scuba diving lessons at the local YWCA.

When a dive club newsletter's notice of a locally sponsored diving contest appeared one month, it caught his interest. His excitement turned to disappointment when he registered and learned that he needed a dive partner for the event. Before he could turn away from the sign-in table, a young man behind him tapped Paul on the shoulder. He offered Paul the chance to dive with him. The object of the event was to retrieve as many brightly colored discs as possible from the Susquehanna River bottom. When the time expired, each team reported their results to be announced at an evening banquet. This young boy and man realized that they had won first prize, an all-expense-paid trip to the Bahamas! These two first place winners made plans to dive in the beautiful underwater heaven of the Caribbean. I noticed a gradual change in his shy demeanor to a more talkative, confident one as a result of this holiday adventure. He eventually became a professional diver.

During this same period, Greg's fleeting high school career was a well-struck balance of academic excellence, athletic successes and lighthearted, youthful fun. Sensitive to my moods even when I hid behind a wall of confidence, Greg's charm and spontaneous wit often lifted my spirits. Later, I realized that my fourth child, in many ways, lived for others instead of himself.

One of the most revealing moments of Greg's desire to please his parents came during his high school graduation speech. Standing before his peers, teachers, administrators and a packed audience, our son spoke of his love for the parents who had stood by him through his life. Only now, I realize that it was Greg who stood by us during those turbulent years. By his 1986 graduation and college enrollment, I was headed for graduate studies at Lincoln University.

Valerie's life was left pretty much unattended, we were too distracted by our own relationship. When I began my professional career, she was the most affected after our close relationship during my final year at community college. As the youngest, Valerie also witnessed my attempts to avoid my marriage. Although I positioned all of our children figuratively between Paul and me, Valerie eventually stood alone in a triangle.

Out of her loneliness and distress, Valerie's true feelings emerged through her poetry. I now realize that her cry for help WAS expressed in her poetry, her only outlet for her true feelings.

By the spring of 1985, while Valerie found her way through her teens, I realized my professional career needed an educational boost. As director, I was hiring court officers who were required to be bachelor degree graduates while I had an associate degree from community college. Although I had taken courses in management and law enforcement, I felt a strong urge to return to academia.

CHAPTER 17

LINCOLN U.

Pennsylvania had recognized the glass ceiling that existed for women and minorities who had been hired in human service agencies during the Affirmative Action Era. This particular group was well qualified from on-the-job training, yet lacked the academic credentials for professional advancement. Pennsylvania's Higher Education Association solicited offers from universities to respond to this group's educational needs. Lincoln University was awarded an accredited Master's Degree in Human Services Program. I was elated when I discovered this program that offered complete degree work within two years, while working and hopefully keeping pace with my children's needs. What I never imagined when registering for the program was the monumental impact that this experience would have on the rest of my life.

Lincoln University's location near Philadelphia was a four hour drive from town. Fortunately, several other area people had registered for the Lincoln program and the four of us agreed to carpool every weekend. Over that two year period, Chuck, Vicky and Stan became not only my travel companions but my mentors and counselors. While I was employed as an administrator, each of them worked directly with clients in several different therapeutic settings. While I was committed to perfectionism for a natural "high", each of them was in recovery from drug and/or alcohol addiction. Their language and philosophy on life sounded so foreign. As I listened, Stan told a story of a teenage life of crime in the inner city, his gradual drug dependency and ultimate freedom from both. Vicky and Chuck, wife and husband, began their life together during the anti-cultural rebellion of the 1960s. They marched for peace and love in Washington, D.C. They traveled across the country as free spirits and drug-addicted souls until they stood at death's door and chose a life of recovery instead. As their Saturday conversations evolved, I found myself feeling closer to these beautiful people than anyone I had ever known. They knew so much more about life's struggles and the human experience than I thought that I would ever learn. I saw myself as a small-town, middle-aged woman who had a normal childhood, uncomplicated adolescence and rewarding adulthood. In the beginning of our companionship, I sympathized with my three co-travelers but grew to envy their commitment to sane and spiritual living while the stress of my own life pressed in from all sides.

My office staff had generously provided encouragement during my studies, so when I sought a volunteer for a required counseling project, Ruth Ann, one of the female employees, readily agreed to become a client. During six one-hour sessions, I listened intently as she revealed a childhood of incest at the hands of her brother-in-law. Her shame and struggling relationships as an adult as well as the self-blame and confusion which continued to stay with her seemed strange yet oddly familiar. That experience combined with an incident on campus, sparked a fire within that smoldered for months.

꧁꧂

The professors in Lincoln's graduate program were all exceptionally skilled professionals in their field. Like the students, they were practitioners during the week and returned to academia every Saturday. One particular professor appeared to have another dimension. As I observed his interaction with students during lectures, I began to wonder if he had the ability to sense others' inner thoughts. He seemed to have an uncanny gift of looking into someone's eyes and drawing out a deep, unconscious communication from the core of that person.

During class once, he recruited me to demonstrate a Gestalt Therapy theory; I was to role play the counselor while another student portrayed the client. Individual counseling techniques, an important component of the Human Services Program, offered various methods of client therapy.

His encouragement bolstered my confidence to participate before a classroom of my peers, all of whom had far more counseling experience than I. Halfway through the scenario, he abruptly interrupted my dialogue to point out my lack of confrontational skills necessary for applying Gestalt theories. Instead, he suggested that my counseling approach resembled a mother breastfeeding an infant.

Humiliation and a growing fear of exposure surfaced, leaving a strangely vulnerable feeling in the presence of this man. It is not the first instance that I recognized this feeling of being helpless and exposed but I could no longer ignore my reaction. His criticism in front of my classmates, so similar to Miss Edward's fourth grade humiliation, needed to be confronted. After recovering from his attack, I spoke privately with him about my suspicion. Could he read my mind in class? Did he know what I was thinking before I knew my own thoughts? He confirmed his gift of insight which he safeguarded constantly from personal misuse. His sincerity relaxed my guard somewhat as I explained how exposed I felt earlier in his classroom. My confusion was global; I was unable to explain any specific reason why my feelings were so strong except for that fourth grade memory.

He suggested that I consider therapy to explore aspects of my own unconsciousness, even offering to make an appointment available in his private practice. But I declined his generosity, indicating to him that my demanding schedule had no more room. Instead, I promised to investigate my feelings after graduation, if they persisted. But during classes at Lincoln University, I did learn to challenge many personal perceptions.

Most of the students in the master's program were from major metropolitan areas like Philadelphia and New York City. Many were of African American decent. I welcomed the opportunity to interact with them since my life experiences were void of connection with black sisters and brothers, although I believed that I was not prejudiced. That myth was dispelled in an instant when a black student stood up in class and spoke intelligently and I had a "chin went to the floor" reaction. I acknowledged my obnoxious attitude and began to correct my beliefs.

Another chance to learn a healthier way of thinking came when the professor directed us to form small groups and identify those clients who we would be unable to counsel. My list included clients who were drug dealers because my teenagers were vulnerable to those menaces. A young male who I had come to respect in our group, looked me in the eye and said, "I am glad you were not the counselor when I sought recovery from drug dealing behavior." The lesson changed my closed-off prejudice again and opened up my reception to clients who sought treatment without judgment. These, as well as many more interactions, were an integral part of a complete education.

From graduation on, both my professional and personal beliefs, values and attitudes of the world's unique individuals were much healthier. The lenses through which I viewed life had changed to a better place.

Throughout the Lincoln experience, my consciousness continued to expand as tiny cracks kept opening up in the deep recesses of my mind; I found it more difficult to explain my reaction. Each time, another powerful explosion of emotion rocked my wall of protection. Violet, one of the feminist professors in the program, gently but effectively jarred me from the uncomplicated and uninvolved living into the dynamic world of personal power as a woman. She introduced many female students to women's strength and values as well as demonstrating the extreme complexities of hierarchy power.

One Saturday remains crystal clear in memory because the effects of Violet's lecture permanently changed my belief system. She cleverly disguised an experiential exercise to simulate cultural classes and stimulate self-awareness. She was truly an artist in exaggerating the obvious impact that power had on individuals. As she divided the class into four groups, she insured that one group would eventually be the powerless, two groups would have minimal privileges, while the fourth would achieve the most powerful control. Then she maneuvered the power masters into the highest authority over the three other groups. This group of participants became abusive toward everyone else by changing all the rules to benefit themselves. I was so enraged at the outcome of this game that I spent hours walking around campus, confused and sobbing deep, gut wrenching cries of pain. My classmates were all human service professionals; I assumed that they were all committed to compassion for other human beings, yet they became so greedy and self-absorbed when given the opportunity to grab power that they lost sight of those who remained powerless under their authority.

My rage exploded after that exercise yet I did not fully understand its implication in my personal life; I did know that my assumptions about others would never again be so naïve. Violet simply smiled gently as I related my total disgust and anger about the exercise. Her insight was far ahead of my own awareness, so she remained silent. I was not quite ready to open the door to my own personal power but Violet made a significant contribution to loosening the hinges.

During the final semester at Lincoln, both a major thesis project on the contribution of women to our country's history and unending hours of documentation drained my energy while my family stood patiently on the sidelines. Two more beautiful grandsons entered our circle as I relentlessly hammered away at my typewriter. Each child warmed my heart as I realized our circle of love was expanding into another generation.

My graduate studies came to an end after my oral presentation in March, 1987. When the celebration and cap-and-gown ceremony were over in May, my life seemed to come to an abrupt halt. The whirlwind stopped so suddenly that I had not prepared myself for the letdown. As I looked around for yet another challenge, I realized that my newfound feminist values no longer felt comfortable within the male dominated court system. I was eager to expand my professional goals now that I had valid credentials behind my name.

Not only changes in my career path but feminist values affected my personal relationship with Paul. This new point of view was a delayed but fulfilling chance to "catch up" with the

1970s Women's Movement, years when my attention was focused on child rearing. However, after Lincoln, I made a commitment to working for social, economic and political equality for women. The change in our relationship as a result of my new world view manifested itself in several ways. For example, I challenged him to rethink his response to a woman walking down the sidewalk. Instead of joining his male coworkers in whistling at her, I explained how disrespectful that behavior was toward her. After some discussion, he adapted in sharing this new perspective, a slight shift in our life together.

CHAPTER 18

NEW CHALLENGE

W ithin three months of graduation, a perfect opportunity arose when the local YWCA advertised for an Executive Director position. I applied with confidence, knowing that my newfound feminine perspective could enhance the women's programs within the YWCA which included a domestic violence crisis center, transitional women's housing program and physical fitness programs customized for women and their families. The selection committee agreed and I was appointed to the director's position.

Like a mother leaving her baby in the hands of strangers, I reluctantly cut the apron strings to the child support enforcement program that I had nurtured for twelve years, no matter that the Lincoln University professor criticized my cradling style. The farewells by staff members included two tributes. They arranged a surprise banquet in my honor, invited my peers from across the state and prepared a program to honor the accomplishments of those years, accomplishments achieved only because of their dedication to the program. Their second generous gift swept me off my feet...literally.

I often told the story of that first nervous Saturday trip to Lincoln; a long four hour, quiet car ride to campus with three strangers. Leaving at 5 A.M., the September light was just beginning to crest the horizon when traveling through Lancaster County farmland. We had just rounded a curve in the highway when the sky filled with colorful hot air balloons rising with the morning sun. That scene lifted my spirits and became a symbol of inspiration during my graduate studies. Remembering that oft told story, the staff presented a musical replica of a hot air balloon and a fantastic two-hour flight in the real thing. Floating weightlessly, high above the earth was a feeling incomparable to any other. Thanks to a thoughtful group of friends and coworkers, I felt the freedom of being suspended in space, immune to restrains, dangers and worries. Many fond memories floated in that sturdy basket transport, career development, professional challenges, personal firsts and agency accomplishments.

Just as the hot air balloons had lifted my spirits while traveling to Lincoln, my spirits soared with the excitement of another challenge. As the newly appointed director of the YWCA, I was confident in my ability to manage this demanding position. Hadn't I achieved statewide recognition for the highest child support collections among Pennsylvania's sixty seven county offices? I had survived the onslaught of months of negative publicity when a staff member was discovered stealing money from clients. What could be more challenging than managing county, state, federal government regulations? I found out all too soon as I settled into the Executive Director's office.

Financial deficits, disorganization among departments, the building's deterioration and poor public relations all demanded immediate attention. I had to admit that even with the challenge of Lincoln University and all of the professional and personal crises, I was not prepared for the complexities of this new challenge.

The Board of Directors' President offered to coordinate my orientation and participation in the National Executive Directors' training scheduled for November of that year. I declined her offer of National YWCA training, since the agency's major funding source, the United Way, had scheduled an annual evaluation during the same weeks. I promised to attend the training program the following year. Another commitment that I delayed during those first few busy months was my annual physical. Originally scheduled for the first week of my new position at the Y, the doctor's office agreed to reschedule the appointment for October.

Although rarely concerned about my health, I did become more attentive to my physical wellbeing after my fortieth birthday. Up until then, neither Paul nor I had maintained an ongoing affiliation with the local medical professionals but we had recently agreed on a physician to commit to annual checkups. The local practitioner was pleasant enough as he reviewed my medical history during that initial visit. I detailed the histories of pregnancy and childbirth complications and past evaluations of fibrocystic breast lumps.

One particularly strange incident had taken place just before Valerie's birth which had alienated me from the local medical community. When I was pregnant with our fifth child, Paul had noticed a lump in my breast which concerned us. When I visited my gynecologist, he immediately contacted a surgeon who scheduled an operation to remove and biopsy the suspicious lump within a week. Fortunately, Barb, a neighbor, suggested I seek out a second opinion at a major medical center located within an hour's drive from us. She had just read an article in Reader's

Digest about the importance of a medical second opinion. I immediately telephoned the Geisinger Medical Center. Relieved by the prompt attention on the other end of the telephone call, I agreed to an appointment 48 hours later. I was told that it would include a thorough examination and several tests.

During the appointment, I listened as a physician explained that the suspicious lumps were an early sign of pregnancy and the prescription was "Go home; there is nothing to worry about". The sweetest words I had heard in a long time.

As a result of this particularly distressing oversight, I had serious doubts about the knee jerk reaction of local physicians and surgeons. What if I would have agreed to the diagnosis and surgery? Would I have put our unborn child in danger? This new family physician listened sympathetically as I recounted this unfortunate incident. His acceptance of my feelings reduced that long held mistrust considerably, but one week later I was once again doubting the local medical community.

CHAPTER 19

LIFE CHANGING EVENT

It all began when my doctor's telephone call interrupted a hectic day at my desk at the YWCA. The minute I heard his voice, I jumped to my feet and literally ran to my office window. I listened to the echo of his words saying that a suspicious area on my breast x-ray concerned him and he recommended an appointment with a local, well qualified surgeon to review the image and provide a further diagnosis. My ears heard the words but I had already escaped the reality and floated far beyond the confines of those four brick walls. I saw myself, robot like, place the telephone on its cradle, return to the chair behind my desk and stare into space in shock, barely breathing. Only a knock on the office door jarred me back into the moment when, once again, I performed as the "perfect" professional, pushing away any reaction to this paralyzing news.

Later that night, in the arms of my husband, I relived aloud the afternoon telephone call. Eventually I agreed to follow through with the doctor's recommendation.

Armed with the mammogram, I consulted with the local surgeon. I went prepared to discuss a course of action which included a needle biopsy that I knew could provide preliminary results before I would consider more radical procedures. The surgeon's negative reaction to my suggestion cemented my decision to return to Geisinger Medical Center for a second opinion. I had given the local physicians an opportunity to dispel my fears and restore my faith but they failed the test. My only hope rested in the alternative; an hour's drive had benefited mother and baby before and now I felt that I was fighting for my life.

A strong feeling of relief washed over me the minute Doctor Diane Leonard walked into the exam room at Geisinger Medical Center. She was petite and lively with a certain aura of compassion. I felt a safety net open up below my weeklong downward spiral. Her recommendation regarding a surgical biopsy paralleled the previous one but she agreed that a needle biopsy would be beneficial. She performed the procedure without hesitation right then while discussing the details of a surgical biopsy. Her willingness to share her professional knowledge and her personal approach to the doctor-patient relationship eased my anxiety. I was able to listen to her explanations. By the end of our meeting, results of the in-office test came back as inconclusive; I agreed to biopsy surgery.

From that moment of decision, two weeks of living in a haze followed before the date of surgery. The possibility of breast cancer was too frightening to consider. Each time that thought pushed through my best efforts to block, I shifted my total concentration on "busy work" as mom defined her activity. Then I understood my mom's use of busy work as a coping skill to avoid fear-past or present.

Even though breast cancer awareness was becoming a public health campaign, even dedicating October as National Breast Cancer Awareness Month, I felt alone in February, 1988. I shut myself away from others, even Paul. As a couple, our communication skills were becoming more and more difficult and this issue was far too volatile to break our sound barrier.

On February 22, 1988, I was just regaining consciousness after surgery while Paul stood vigilant by my side in the recovery room when Dr. Leonard approached. Although my mind was still cloudy, a very clear message flashed like lightning bolts through the fog. I HAD BREAST CANCER. There was a monster invading my body and its name was cancer. I immediately closed my emotional walls and asked the doctor for as much literature on breast cancer as she had available. Within minutes she returned; her arms were laden with books from her personal library. I was determined to learn as much as possible to help me make one of the most important decisions of my life. She graciously recommended taking as much time as I needed to decide on the next medical procedure. She refrained from further discussion as I eased back on the litter and buried myself in hospital white sheets and thermal blankets. I suddenly felt a chill shudder through my body from head to toe. Eventually I slept in silence for another hour until my body's warmth returned. Paul and I said very little after receiving that shocking news; I was already buried in a medical book to begin to face the reality which had not yet fully impacted my consciousness.

For the next six weeks, I struggled with the multitude of problems at the YWCA while I wrestled with life and death at night. Books on breast cancer were strewn everywhere in the house. Whenever I sat down, I needed access to black words on a white page, never a pause to allow feelings. Insomnia plagued my struggle, too, so whenever I couldn't sleep, I journalized on lined pages of a small pink covered booklet.

The entire self-absorption was frightening to loved ones. They misinterpreted my isolation. To them, I was completely avoiding my illness. They were afraid, watching helplessly from the sidelines. I refused to open up those solid walls of security long enough for them to realize my own internal turmoil of fear. I kept my feelings so well hidden that one of my adult children became desperate and approached my local doctor for some information. He betrayed our patient-doctor confidentiality by talking without permission. I was furious; I felt violated. This was MY body, MY breast; I was the only one who had to deal with the consequences of my cancer. I selfishly thought that everyone needed to leave me alone to wrestle with this monster. After all, only I would decide if I would lose a breast to save my life. The more anger that surfaced during those six weeks, the more determined I was to do battle with cancer on my terms.

Armed with new understanding after weeks of digesting books written by and for breast cancer survivors, I demanded bone scans and additional tests to aid in my decision making. If any indication of cancer invasion beyond the lump in my right breast was evident, then I decided that a mastectomy would be fruitless. If nothing suspicious appeared in the test results, then a radical mastectomy offered the best and quickest recovery option.

The bone scan and blood tests proved beneficial and hopeful; there was no indication of cancer elsewhere in my body. Dr. Leonard and I agreed on a radical mastectomy and a breast implant. The plastic surgeon thoroughly explained the implant procedure. I was anxious to resume my normal life as soon as possible. No radiation, no chemotherapy, no clumsy bra inserts to fumble with; no visible announcement that my female body or perfect lifestyle was marred. Breast cancer treatment during the 1980s did not require further radiation or chemotherapy for a radical mastectomy when there was no spread of cancer cells.

The day of surgery was a blur except for the drive to the hospital. Every minute of that journey seemed like an eternity and each mile pulled me closer to my final battleground with the Monster. During that drive, a large bird of prey suddenly flew across the highway in front of our car. As I watched it swoop with a full wingspread, I thanked my spirit guide for the sign of power. I too was capable of spreading my own wings to confront the enemy and attack it fearlessly. A peaceful assurance of victory; I breathed deeply for the first time since Paul and I began our drive that morning. From then on I was occupied with all the details of presurgery preparations, the hours of a lengthy operation, the fight back from anesthesia. The monster had been conquered; no invasion beyond my right breast. I was the victor so I thought.

Later that week, I received a letter from our daughter Lorraine.

dear mom,

How are you feeling? Dad said that you were pretty much out of it after surgery. That many hrs. of surgery can really exhaust anyone. But knowing my mom-she won't let this get the best of her. The fighter in her will be up and at 'em again before they have a chance to miss her.

I wish I could visit so I could help you and also we could sit and talk and catch up on our lives. Some times life seems to go so quickly that I feel I've lost something. I look back and it seems so long ago and maybe I didn't see it the way I do looking back, know what I mean?

Yes, Lorraine, I do.

Paul remained supportive throughout those following weeks, even bravely changing the surgical bandages daily where my right breast had been. There was only one brief moment when we clashed. One evening after supper, he announced that he needed to move out for a while. My anger exploded into rage as I pounded on the kitchen table where we sat. I stood up with all the force I could gather and with fire in my eyes, I looked into his eyes, loudly announcing "if you leave now, everyone will know that you abandoned a woman with one breast."

When my anger subsided, I realized that Paul's fear was genuine. Both his parents had died from cancer and now his wife was being threatened by the same killer. His experience with cancer always translated into the death of a loved one; his fight-or-flight response had kicked in to protect him from any further painful loss. I quickly apologized for my ignorance.

After that explosive episode, we were able to communicate more openly; we talked about his feelings and concerns more easily while I remained closed off for several more months. During that time, my journaling continued. Through the daily pages of revealing my inner most thoughts, a reality was becoming clear. I needed help coping with volumes of strong emotions that were pushing against the stone walls of safety that I had built for forty-six years.

CHAPTER 20

THE VOICE

An early 1988 journal entry

How could everything change yet remain the same? The answer eluded the early morning journal writer. The soft light of dawn silhouetted her bent frame at the kitchen table. Her handwritten words raced across the pages of her private journal. She wondered about many events, both now and then, in new ways. Fred's death, so sudden, so shocking, leaving her alone to raise two small babies. Were these factors contributing to her inability to recall events before his death? Or were there other reasons for lost memories? Twenty-three years ago, she accepted the lost memories as God's gift of protection from her overwhelming grief. Now she wasn't so certain about that conclusion. In fact, she wasn't sure about anything that morning. She was still reeling with shock from last week's surgery. The songs of birds outside the kitchen window were the same as yesterday but she was different today. She stared into the face of death and that face changed everything else. What she accepted as a welcome relief was no longer acceptable. She had even ignored her discomfort at high school class *reunions when everyone laughed and joked when they recalled teen memories and she didn't join in their conversations. The finality of death brought an urgency to bear on important matters. Her two oldest children deserved to know their biological father's life with them. She was the only one to tell them that story. Until now, there was no urgency, no reason to recall the past. That changed.*

The tone of my journal entries changed, too, over the months as uncomfortable feelings oozed out between the cracks in my internal fortress. Writing helped connect to myself. As I opened the pages of the journal and just let mind and spirit connect on each white page, my awareness grew. I continued to administer the YWCA's operations but with less and less enthusiasm. Even after Dr. Leonard's assurance that the cancer had been completely eradicated, I still feared a monster could be eating away inside without any means of detecting its destruction.

Gerry Spence wrote, "When we engage in the physical act of writing, a connection is struck between the hands and that portion of the brain where our creative powers are stored, so that we are more likely to produce a new idea while we write or type than while we engage in the simple act of thinking alone." The magic of writing guided my journey through discovery.

Journey entry excerpt:

I'm shaky and tense and I don't know why. I wake up thinking about things at work that have put a lot of pressure yet it seems like I am forcing myself to think about work to avoid dealing with the things in my personal life that matter. How does that feel? I feel scared. I know there are so many more things that I have been forced to do that made me feel frightened and I want to relive them for my own health but I shy away from the very opportunities I have to get in touch with them. I'm frustrated because my legs are tense and jumpy and I can't get in touch with the reasons I feel that way. Last night when Paul and I were sitting in the living room watching a video tape about relationships, I noticed that the man's voice caused tension. After awhile I couldn't take anymore. Then we watched a movie about a female lawyer and a male judge who was seeking out prostitutes and was manipulating the lawyer during a trial. I was upset with him.

Earlier, dad was here and I had a problem looking him in the eye and the same with my mom. There are new feelings and awareness that I have about them and I'm not yet comfortable with them. I wish I could just talk to dad and tell him that it was very hard while I was growing up because they created a triangle and I competed for his attention with my mother. That both of them were adults, yet I was subjected to this bizarre situation. I want to tell him that I love him and don't want to hurt him but have to deal with my past so I can get on with my present and future. I want to tell him there are some things that I don't know about yet. I want him to tell me how he feels and listen to him talk. For once in my life, I want to hear my father's voice and know that he is speaking without my mother's interference. I understand if he can't do that; it may be something he doesn't want to do or can not do. Daddy, just hang in there and the pain will subside and we'll be okay. Right now I can't explain everything and understand the *implications but gradually it will all fall in place and we'll have a better, healthier relationship.*

April 14, 1988's journal entry:

Paul has been so wonderful and I am having a hard time dealing with his love. I want to reject it and protect myself from him getting too close. I find myself pushing away from him when he is so loving and gentle. His tenderness is what I need the most but these are the moments that are the scariest. I panic. I don't want anyone to be angry. I am sorry I didn't mean to hurt you. I don't know what to do but, I promise, I'll try never to push away. I just want someone to love, hold and carry me off in safety to someplace where I can live without pain. That place would have open fields and a sparkling pond. The waters of the pond would be soothing to my legs and back. The water would gently swirl around my body and gradually release the tension. The color of water would change to red as my tension leaves my body. The red would fade into the blue of warmth and I would feel strength and energy take the place of pain. I would be pure and without stain.

The voice that was immerging in my journal entries helped to realize that my workaholic energy kept me distant from Paul. It's no wonder that he felt left out. I prayed that our life together would become more stable and I could become more in tune with his needs. The subject of sex reminded me that he felt cheated. Paul's remarks on the subject included the statement that married men turn to prostitutes for sexual satisfaction. I wasn't sure he meant it as a threat or just state that he aligned himself with men who seek intimacy outside their marriage. I didn't really want to analyze his motives; I wanted to love him with all my heart and soul.

Another entry in April when beginning to address God in my conversation:

Today God, my body aches from work yesterday but I'm okay because You were here. The exercises to strengthen my arm from the surgery left me tired but I feel good that I was still awake when Paul came to bed. I know with your help I'll make it thru these rough edges. I start again in making today as full and as rewarding as possible. Help me not to forget my first love Paul. I want to touch his heart and body so gently and lovingly that he will know without doubt that I love him totally and completely.

I was preparing for a second surgery, a gel breast implant. Weekly trips to Geisinger for saline injections into an expander to stretch my chest muscles to accept the permanent implant. Although my writings rarely mentioned this procedure, it was an added dimension to this period.

Good morning Goddess, the sunrise starts with such serenity and a quiet greeting into a new and challenging sunrise. Occasionally I wonder where I will be led; just what my role here in this place is to mean. for awhile now, I realize that your plans include a certain path, however, the details still are not known. Sometimes I long to look ahead with excitement but just knowing that you are walking with me is excitement enough, knowledge enough for now. I begin again with joy and a grateful heart.

During 1988 after several months of daily journaling, a clearer vision of spiritual growth and purpose evolved.

Welcome into my heart Goddess, since I've started writing in the mornings to you, I've begun to feel your spirit in my life more fully. I look forward to writing because I realize the words aren't always mine but you speak through this time we spend together.

How do I serve you? **by being faithful, truthful, loving and caring.** I must begin with Paul. You sent him in my darkest hour of need and he holds the keys to your way. Let me never be so blind that I don't see the gifts that are given with such determination and wisdom.

Good morning God, I have struggled with my awareness of feminism and I see both sides of life a little fuller. I still don't understand why the church dwells so completely on masculine power. Power for good has to be without gender, otherwise what hope do women have of understanding their independent, direct contact with you as one who wears neither a masculine nor feminine mantle?

Dear God, I think I'm on the right track and then something else stands in the way. Well, yesterday I really felt defeated for awhile. I even thought about just disappearing. The feeling passed but it was so real that it was frightening. Touch me now as I pass through this season and place with conviction and determination to meet my master along the pathway. Your gentleness is woman, your strength is man. You are two in one with the best of both sexes amplified in your spirit.

5/19/88 good morning God. I feel I must be doing more, giving more. I guess I am expecting to hear a voice. That's just because of my human experience and my limitations. I want to believe that it is you who writes the words on the pages and it is your voice that speaks thru my writings. I mean it is difficult to think that you really come even when the entire world calls to you and needs your attention.

I am able to be everywhere all the time. Whenever and wherever my children call my name, I am there to soothe their fears and wipe away their tears.

Excerpts... The other day in the woods when the red leaves fell all around, your message was that the blood must be shed for your sake. Life will be lost before I am restored to a place of love and joy.

Create in me a new heart; one that is full of compassion and understanding for those around me. You will be my guide and my strength through the journey that lies ahead.

come dance with me today and every day of your life. Sing a song of joy, sing praises to my name. begin to teach my message to those around you so that they too may sing my praises and know my ways. Keep vigil over the morning and I will come to you when you are ready. I know the time, stand ready and you will be able to follow me. Begin now to clear the way for my arrival. Sweep away the cobwebs and dust from your feet and stand tall so

I will know that your strength is lasting and you are ready for the journey.

No one will be free to choose their path—no one ever has. I have always been the one who decides the way. I now am telling you to follow without hesitation, without reservation, without questions for I will provide all that your soul will need, all that your spirit requires and all that your body needs to serve me. You will never tire when my work is to be done. You will have the strength of hundreds and the wisdom of thousands if you just place your trust in me. Together we are about to begin.

PART 2

CHAPTER 1

SEARCH FOR ANSWERS

I sat quietly now, desperately trying to regain control of an inner whirlwind of emotion. What was happening? Why was I shaking uncontrollably? What was this stinging feeling? It had been a typical evening in June, 1988. My parents, my husband Paul and I had been sitting around the kitchen table, recounting childhood memories. Suddenly, I felt a burst of pain. I ran from the kitchen into the safety of my bedroom where I sat fighting to regain composure.

I could still hear those frightening words, "YOU HAVE BREAST CANCER". From that moment in December 1987, my life changed forever. I kept thinking about cancer. Even after successful surgery, I still feared this enemy. This monster could be eating away at my body while I worked, slept or played and I had no control over its invisible destruction. Even after I resumed my daily routine, I continued to be preoccupied with the fear of dying from cancer.

As I contemplated this creature called cancer and my possible death, I realized that there was some unfinished business in my life. There were vast periods when I had no memory! I could not remember anything prior to my first husband's death. Since his death, I had rationalized that my memory loss was God's way of creating a safe path to today and tomorrow. But after my bout with cancer, yesterday **was** important. Since my tomorrows carried the possibility of death, my roots and my past took on more meaning.

In August of 1988, I sought the guidance of a female therapist in Lewisburg, a nearby community. Although I was eager to regain my memories, I felt the need to protect my privacy in my own town. As I still greatly valued my roles of executive director, wife and mother extraordinaire, I refused to risk the stigma surrounding psychotherapy that might result in a blemish to my perfect image. In describing perfectionism, author Anne Lamott explained that our psychic muscles *"cramp around our wounds-the pain from our childhood, the losses and disappointments of adulthood, the humiliation suffered in both-to keep us from getting hurt in the same place again, to keep foreign substances out. Perfectionism is one way our muscles cramp. In some cases we don't even know that the wounds and the cramping are there, but both limit us."*

Caroll, a feminist therapist, listened intently as I explained the dilemma which brought me to therapy. As I discussed the impact that cancer had on my life and the urgency I felt in being able to remember my past, especially before my first husband was killed in an automobile crash. Caroll's undivided attention eased my uncertainty in talking to a stranger. I had rehearsed over and over again what I would say during that initial counseling session. When I found her practice listed in the yellow pages as a feminist therapist, I relaxed somewhat since my own beliefs were based on newfound feminine principles.

Together, we established goals for possibly uncovering lost memories, beginning with a focus on what I did remember. She also strongly recommended group therapy in addition to our individual sessions each week. Reluctantly I agreed to both, even though I told her that I had nothing to contribute to the group.

I was sure the other participants had far more serious problems than my simple memory loss. What I did not realize then was the significance that the other group members would have in my discovery process. After the first Wednesday night group session, I awoke the next morning to find myself lying upside down in my bed, perhaps ominous that my world was about to turn upside down...and inside out.

During the first few counseling sessions, Caroll recommended that I record dreams. She explained that dreams provide the avenue of unconsciousness. One vivid dream did emerge early in treatment yet it seemed confusing as I relayed the details to my counselor.

I was standing on the beach at the water's edge, a small young girl stood at my left side, an older woman on my right. The older woman explained the dangers of going back on the shoreline path. As I turned around, I noticed small vicious monsters scattered along the pathway. I watched in horror as our family dog Lady tried to reach my side but instead was devoured by these creatures. I resolved to plunge into the water ahead, even though I knew that unknown dangers may be lurking beneath the water's surface. I refused to retreat to the path which had brought me to the water's edge. I held hands with the young girl and the wise woman and the three of us dove into the deep dark water before us. The dream's message to continue exploring the unknown became clearer as I finished relating it to Caroll.

A journal entry during those first counseling sessions also was revealing.

Open yourself up with guards standing on either side of the doorway. They will watch and protect you from the voids and evils. They will only let kindness and love pass through to within your opened doors. They will guard against those who mean to harm you or those who don't even see you as they try to pass through. The guards are your wisdom and pain experienced in your years gone by. Their eyes are wise and penetrate the souls of those who seek entrance. They can protect and guide your soul from harm. They recognize the good from evil. Give yourself over to them and trust their judgment. They are you in the early years. They are strong now and can be trusted to save you from more pain.

The importance of my participation in a group gradually grew as each member contributed to the overall development of trust. My walls of safety loosened as I realized that these women could be trusted to respect my feelings, validate my thoughts and return respect and trust by sharing their deepest emotions and personal trials.

During an emotional session, when Susan discussed the pain of her father's abusive acts during her childhood, other members were visibly moved to tears. Caroll's voice "Rosemary, what are you feeling?"

Without hesitation, I responded, "Numb." Immediately I realized that numbness is the absence of feeling; it's not a feeling. Instantly, I flashed to other times and places when numbness described my feelings. When Fred died, from the moment of the phone call through hours, days, weeks in the aftermath, I remained numb. But in that group circle, a wellspring of tears burst open and I sobbed deep moans of pain.

Without a spoken word between us, the group knew that my buried pain had surfaced. Their support made the release possible. Before the session ended that evening, Joyce offered to follow me on the highway because she recognized my shattered state. My knee-jerk reaction was a typical one. "No thanks, I'm fine" I said when actually I didn't want to inconvenience her. The highway drive would have meant an extra hour for her since she lived only a few blocks from Caroll's office. Besides, I felt unworthy of such generosity, undeserving of such attention from anyone. I was already uncomfortable with the show of affection from these wonderful women earlier during my emotional outpouring.

But within five minutes behind the wheel on the four lane highway home, I wished Joyce was behind. As headlights blinded my vision and cars sped past I felt unnerved, frightened and strangely exposed. Although I was an excellent driver and usually enjoyed the privacy and freedom of these drives to and from the therapy sessions, I could barely function. That night I imagined Joyce following close behind as my personal escort until I parked in our garage, raced in the back door and through the kitchen to collapse in Paul's arms on the couch. He held me until the shaking stopped, then encouraged me to share what had caused this reaction. In generalities, I related the group incident and the challenge of that difficult drive .

After that initial realization of pain, the tone of my journal entries and one-hour sessions changed.

My dream: I have a sense of a cellar door and I'm trying to close it but there is a monster or a blob forcing it open. Even oozing out around the edges of the door. I don't have enough strength to force the door closed. Is anger my monster that oozes around the door? That can't be locked up anymore? I must open that door soon I will not be able to keep it out. I want to experience the full range of its rage. I know I will have to be prepared for its full force but I imagined that the release would be wonderful. I'll be free of its grip forever.

Days hold moments of roller coaster feelings of being lightheaded and confused. Yesterday a woman who I respected was suffering. She had breast cancer surgery and had discovered a lump in her neck that the doctor was going to watch for six weeks before making a recommendation. I held her in my arms and cried with her as she dealt with the fear of not knowing. I felt strong enough to tell her that I wanted to be her friend and she accepted.

In group I asked for help in developing this new friendship. I was afraid I would again push another person away. During the group session I did feel something as Mary described her emotional relationship with another woman. She described it with such tenderness that I found myself feeling a longing, an ache for a relationship like she described. When the other women held hands at the end of our session, I felt their energy and warmth. It filled my being as I drove home holding on to that peaceful feeling hoping I could make it last.

I responded to Paul that night with that same warmth. His touches relaxed my guard. I wanted to surrender to his tenderness. He touched my breast and I immediately pulled away. I thought I saw another man and I was scared. My legs jumped uncontrollably, my stomach tightened and I wanted to run away.

CHAPTER 2

THE WIDOW'S MEMORIES

Over a period of several sessions with Caroll I focused on putting together scattered scenes of moments surrounding Fred's death. I remembered the phone call in the middle of the night…then a house full of family and friends…I saw myself dressed in black walking behind a pearl white casket. It was like watching a movie in slow motion. Standing alone in the backyard staring up at a star filled sky and the only words on my lips and in my heart was, "WHY?"

With Caroll's questions, "What happened next?" "How did you feel?" and asking for more details. "Where were you when that happened?" "Was the temperature warm or cold?" "What were you wearing?", memories and flashbacks of Fred's death did emerge, accompanied by inexplicable physical reactions. Silent streams of tears, loud moans, pangs of stomach cramps, chills from head to toe gradually matched the memories. Caroll explained the importance of connecting feelings with each flash from the past. When my shoulders twitched with unexplained pressure, visions of standing at the kitchen sink with water overflowing a coffee pot flooded my senses. I screamed in terror. It wasn't a bad dream after all.

❧

I was telling Caroll that the "whys" had been haunting for weeks after Fred's death. It was then that I sought the advice of our parish priest Father Ulrich. After all, I said, this man of God was my instructor of the Catholic faith before I was married. He officiated at our wedding and he heard my confessions every week or so.

I scheduled his visit one afternoon while my two little children napped so we could talk without interruption. Our conversation was less than satisfying; his comments about God's plan for each person didn't satisfy my agony. My frustration couldn't be contained so I stood up from the kitchen table where we sat and offered to make him a cup of coffee. I wanted to scream but reasoned that he tried to answer my questions within the realm of his religion.

While I watched the crystal clear water from the kitchen sink slowly fill the coffee pot, my mind was somewhere else. I thought about how often I filled that same coffee pot at dinner time just a few weeks ago for my beloved. I barely heard the kitchen chair slide away from the table, hardly noticed his black leather shoes step across the linoleum floor. Then suddenly his arms encircled my body from behind, his hands cupped my breasts and he was pushing his body against mine, trapping me between the cold porcelain sink and him. I felt his hot breath as he whispered in my left ear. "I know what you REALLY need."

I couldn't believe his strange behavior; my mind went blank as he turned me around to face him. This man was not the same priestly counselor that had taught religion; it was another man with evil in his eyes and this overpowering creature led me down the hallway to my bedroom. I didn't pull away; I couldn't scream because my daughter and son would wake and I couldn't escape. This evil man disguised as a priest forced me onto my marriage bed. He towered over my body, forced my clothes off and exposed himself. With brutal force, he raped me.

The reality of finally facing the truth was freeing. I died inside that day, walking through life like a robot. I had no feelings, just a mask of smiles to hide behind, never emerging from the depths, buried under secrets, unable to breathe fresh air, just pretending.

Caroll gently and slowly provided guidance through the onslaught of memories that continued unfolding. As I watched myself being forced onto my marriage bed by that rapist, I felt rage erupt like daggers from deep inside. I imagined thrusting them into the hearts of priests, God, religion, and men that were my personal betrayers. As I relived that horrific trauma from twenty four years earlier, I realized the complete destruction of my body, mind and spirit committed by this criminal. I was determined to seek reparation.

Following therapy that week, I composed a letter to the priest after locating him within the diocese. The letter informed him of my memory loss following his crime, the recent discovery of his violent rape and my determination to expose him for his actions. I also forwarded two copies of the letter, one to the diocese bishop and another to Father Clark, a former parish priest that I had respected and trusted.

The letter was dated February 24, 1989.

"Rev. Carl Ulrich,

Today as I remember the injustice you did, I can no longer keep silent. In February, 1965 my husband was killed in a tragic car accident. As our parish priest, you were there to provide consolation and prayers. Two weeks after the tragedy you visited under the pretext of offering spiritual guidance but instead you raped me. You forced yourself and sexually assaulted me in my bedroom. You then arranged for a private confession so no one would ever know.

Well, I know! I have carried the pain of that act for years and refuse to any longer. It was you who used your power and position to gain access and took advantage of that power at my weakest moment. For half my life, the weight of your violence has been on my soul and I am now free of the pain. I only have rage and anger left and my voice. That silence is broken and you are now the one who must answer for your brutality."

Once the letters were mailed I had difficulty functioning. There were moments when my legs ached, others when my head felt so dizzy that I was afraid of passing out. I fought to stay focused on the demands at hand. I was afraid of my reaction to the priest letter. I thought that Father Clark would likely be the mediator of my letter. I imagined that he would be told by the bishop to investigate the matter and protect the church at all costs. I thought that I would tell Clark that what the church does with Ulrich is their business. But with thinking more about my response, I really wanted the church to strip him of his office and ban him from any authority. His evil acts violated everything that he represented as a leader of a church. The abuse of his power within the sanctity of a worldwide organization of faith was disgusting. Under the cloak of piety, this rapist manipulated those of us who trusted the man of God. The shadow of unsuspecting, vulnerable youngsters and adults who became his victims were standing beside me as I prepared to confront the bastard. I was certain that he had attacked others.

Within one week, Father Clark called to say that the criminal rapist was anxious to meet to apologize for his crime.

"When I am ready to confront the bastard, I will let you know. Until then, let him feel the pain that he inflicted." I slammed the telephone down. My response was spontaneous. The decision to confront my rapist was clear.

The following journal writings began with four statements. "I feel, I think, I fear and I want."

I think I have carried this monkey on my back too long. I feel numb because I have denied myself the opportunity to fully experience the pain of this rape. I am angry because I am unable to free myself of this old functioning. I want to have the ability to release myself of this behavior. I think that the first step in opening myself to the experience is to validate the feelings I do have that I pulled into myself.

I feel shock. you came with such force, I was forced against my will to submit to your demands. I feel anger at my inability to resist your demands. I hadn't even allowed myself to feel the full range of sorrow over my husband's death and I sure as hell wasn't going to deal with this attack. Who would be able to anyway? I cried out to my God and you came. You came to rob me of my only hope to feel peace of mind and spirit. When you attacked, I could no longer rely on anyone or anything ever again. Your actions left me with nothing but myself to depend on. I feel sadness for this young widow. She was so hoping for an answer from you that made sense out of her husband's tragic death and you just raped her. She was full of want and sorrow and you didn't respond with compassion. You showed her your penis instead.

I love that young innocent woman because she had been devastated yet she still clung to hope. She did what she could to survive. What she did was stop feeling, stop experiencing, stop living. She gave herself messages that someone sometime would treat her with love and understanding but she couldn't love herself. She just waited patiently while not allowing herself to feel. She couldn't feel. My god, that would be too dangerous. She might be hurt again and she couldn't risk that danger. She remained buffered by her walls of self defense. That would see her through.

Each of my weekly afternoon counseling sessions pinpointed each detail of what I wanted from the important face-to-face meeting with my rapist. A series of questions and answers became the basis of my sessions.

* WHAT DO I HOPE TO GAIN FROM THIS CONFRONTATION?
* WHAT ARE MY MOTIVES?
* WHAT DO I STAND TO LOSE?
* DO I HAVE A SOLID ENOUGH SUPPORT SYSTEM?
* AM I STABLE AND CENTERED ENOUGH TO RISK BEING CALLED CRAZY?

I am not sure. I stayed centered when I risked talking to Ulrich on the telephone. I kept hearing him say how he was affected by my letter and was anxious to meet right away, even though I had already told him that it would probably be at least another month before the meeting was set up. He said "you started this by writing the letter"

"Oh, no I didn't, you started this 24 years ago when you raped me"

The best outcome of my meeting will be that I am honest about the feelings I had when he raped me. That I can verbalize all the true reality of that attack in all its trauma and fear. I am more aware of my feelings now and have the ability and the support of myself and others to work through the pain rather than deny its existence. I will be alright. I am woman. I am strong and full of life.

While Caroll and I prepared for the confrontation, members of our therapy group provided constant support while Paul's loving arms countered the nightmares of fear and out of control feelings which invaded our bedroom.

I also sought legal advice, only to learn that Pennsylvania's statutes of limitation on rape had long expired. The attorney offered to challenge the statute by appealing any lower court's decision. I decided to continue my plans for a direct confrontation rather than put myself and my family through the added trauma of public trials through the courts up to and including the Pennsylvania Supreme Court. It was at that point, I also made a personal decision to pen my memoirs as an encouragement for other sexual abuse survivors and to give voice to my own traumas.

On May 1st, 2002 I did publicly give voice to my sexual violation by writing a letter to the Editor of our local newspaper.

"Editor, Sun-Gazette: the media focus on sexual abuse by clergy lifts a veil of secrecy from these horrible crimes. I add my voice to this issue in an effort to shed light also on the assaults of young adults by those we called "father."

At 22 years old, I suddenly became a widow because my husband had died in an auto accident. Through my shock and confusion, I reached out for spiritual guidance. Instead, I was raped by a trusted priest in my own bedroom while my two young children slept in the next room.

The crime of religious incest destroys much in its wake for many. My losses of clear mind, body and spirit were replaced with numbness from faith, hope and love for many years.

For all who know the pain of sexual assault by clergy, you are not alone."

The headline of my letter was captioned "Crime of Religious Incest".

Three months passed before I felt prepared for the confrontation with my rapist. May 18th, 1989 was the date I chose. Later, I discovered my journal entry of May 18th, 1988 - exactly one year- *God, what is it that I must do to open my ears clearly to your voice? Must I continue to wait until You chose the time of the message. If so, I am ready whenever You decide.*

I selected a conference room in a women's center on Bucknell University campus as the site of the meeting, the same campus where I presented my Lincoln Thesis. I spent hours designing the seating arrangements, lighting and other details in the room to secure a sense of safety for myself. Every item of my clothing and jewelry was selected for this same purpose.

Then at group counseling on the night before my scheduled meeting, each of my cherished friends offered a symbol which I would carry into the meeting. The amazing thing about those gifts was the strength that I felt from them. They all promised to meet as a group following the afternoon event. They also spoke of Amazon Women, like me, chose to cut off their right breast to better aim their bow and arrows at the enemy. I also learned that thousands of women in Alabama have adopted this fierce tribe of survivors as a model for their own lives. These warrioresses, these breast cancer survivors, had found weapons to fight and survive: faith, courage, community, science, rage, education and power.

Caroll, along with another counselor who specialized in sexual abuse, agreed to accompany me to the meeting. I had notified the priest of the date and place but was unsure whether he would be alone or accompanied by others.

Although Paul had remained steadfastly by my side throughout my recovery, he had personal conflicts with the criminal. This same priest had been Paul's high school basketball monitor and had celebrated several successful seasons with him during Paul's sports career. I could appreciate his struggle to reconcile his positive memories of this athletic and religious leader with the anguish he felt about the criminal rapist in priest's garb whom I was about to confront. I encouraged him to accompany me to the site but remain in a private area next to the conference room.

The day arrived. I was filled with nervous energy as I watched the clock tick off minutes toward 3 P.M.

It was a dark pink shirtwaist dress with short sleeves and side pockets. I referred to this outfit as my power dress because I chose it for one of those important moments in my life. There was a navy blue suit for my first wedding; a pink gown for my second walk down the aisle. In each event, the importance of what I wore reflected how I felt. The soft flowing gown that I chose when Paul and I married reflected the start of a new life.

That morning as I soaked in the warmth of an herbal bath surrounded by scented candles, my thoughts of gratitude for others' love and support swelled my heart. Several gifts from the counseling group were laying on my dresser. I slipped on my dress, lit a red candle for courage, fastened a crystal necklace at my throat for clarity and slipped a small pocketknife into my dress pocket for protection. My grandmother's beautiful gold bracelet was the final symbol of strength that I chose. Even though she had died in 1973, her courageous spirit would offer a powerful energy now. The bracelet's inscription of dates and initials of a legacy of women beginning with 1885 would carry the strength of all these women. A beautiful card with a loving message from Paul was the last item to carry to this important meeting. His handwritten message; "I know you will survive because you are a survivor. Love always, Paul."

I planned to be at the women's center an hour ahead of schedule to review any last minute details. I anticipated arriving before my attacker but as Paul and I walked into the center, the priest was seated on a bench across the lobby. As he glanced in our direction, I froze in fear. Paul's arms led the way into a room where Caroll was waiting for us. By then my whole body was shaking out of control at the mere sight of the man who had robbed me of a healthy life. The shock of my own reaction was followed by anger. The energy of that anger surged forth from every cell of my body. I walked into a nearby restroom, stood at a mirror and had a conversation with myself.

"Rosemary, you have committed four grueling months to prepare for this moment. Don't blow it now. This monster is simply a helpless old man who has no more power over you now." The face in the mirror drew strength from the voice of the survivor, "You are ready now to slay the monster." My shoulders squared, my legs felt firmly grounded, my heart's pounding had calmed and I was breathing deeply again. I exited the restroom to the hall where Caroll and Paul were anxiously waiting. Paul embraced me with the warmth of his arms and heart. We walked together the short distance to the room where he would remain during my confrontation. As I kissed Paul gently on the cheek, I thanked him for his deep and constant love which had sustained us through the turmoil. Then I turned to face one of the greatest battles of my life.

CHAPTER 3

VICTORY

S atisfied that all the planning was in place, I took my position in the conference room. Caroll escorted the man dressed in black into the room. The red candle flickered as he took his seat across the table from me. I chose the power position in the room, my chair at the end of the conference table facing the door, without giving the criminal any easy escape. Behind me were several large windows where the afternoon sun warmed my back while my shadow darkened his face. Caroll and Judy, the other counselor, sat on either side of me. I began speaking those well rehearsed words slowly and deliberately.

"Today is my opportunity to speak openly about your crime and its affects on my life for twenty-four years. Fred's death in 1965 was in many ways my death, too. You will not interrupt until I am finished."

" I was a young woman who loved life, believed in the goodness of others, full of hope and joy. I praised my God for blessings. I was so happy. I had two beautiful children, a son and daughter. I had the perfect life: a wonderful, handsome husband and a home that I took pride in caring for and reflecting love."

"I lost my joy in living; I lost my happiness. I lost my belief in a god; I lost my trust in everyone. When you raped me, I died a painful death. I was still walking, talking, moving from minute to minute but each movement brought deep pain. I numbed that pain so it didn't hurt to walk, to talk, to move. I plastered on a false face-an ever present smile-with a dead body and dead eyes. I buried my young, handsome husband and myself when I was violated." The words rolled off my tongue just as I had scripted.

" You raped me when I had no defenses to fight back." I felt a burst of fear between my legs. I slipped my hand into my dress pocket where I found the knife and curled my fingers tightly around the cool metal weapon.

"You stole my body, my God, my soul. I spent the last twenty-four years fighting against the memory and terror of that day. I pulled the walls of protection up so tightly that no one could ever penetrate again. Your crime denied me intimacy and happiness. In addition, my husband, children and friends suffered the loss of my love and trust not knowing why."

The criminal at the other end of the table began to defend himself and I saw fire. I immediately jumped to my feet and shouted, "No more! I'm not finished." He silently sank deeper into the rigid aluminum chair that I chose for his prosecution.

"My life has been barren and lonely. My constant wish to be perfect clashed repeatedly with my deep, unconscious death wish. Only now I understand the complexity of the pain you inflicted. You even used the power of the church to insist that I go to confession to your chosen priest who conspired to keep your crime secret. What you did not plan on was that your crime was not so easily forgiven. I WAS NOT the sinner even though you convinced me that I was while I lived with the shock of my husband's death and your rape. Now you will pay for your crime on my terms or I assure you that the news of your crime will be on my lips until this entire community is told," I said.

An apology to me and to any other females that he most likely sexually violated was one of my demands. I also wanted to attend a program for sexual assault victims abused by Catholic priests in the Milwaukee Diocese, the only program available of its kind.

He quietly read over the written list; he then agreed to sign the document that was before him. His voice quivered as he spoke the words of apology with his head dropped and his eyes looking downward. My power had escalated during the past hour to the point of arrogance. "Look at me when you say you are sorry," I shouted.

When he, the shadow of a man, left the room, the victory celebration began. I laughed, cried, danced, hugged Caroll, then dashed into the next room to embrace Paul. The anxiety left his face as I burst into his arms, still laughing, crying and celebrating this newfound freedom and power. Within an hour, I was surrounded by the group who joined the celebration as they listened eagerly to the details of the meeting. As I returned each member's treasure which had been so significant earlier, the connection that I felt with these women entered my heart and still remains intact. I truly felt worthy of others' affection.

Later I expressed my gratitude for Paul's affection. The greeting card was entitled "With love, for you." followed by:

"We've been through a lot together since our wedding vows when we promised for better, for worse and we both know how bad the 'for worse' can be. But I think that one of the best 'for better' parts is that we have faced it-all of it-together. I am full of new feelings today and many are for you. I am so grateful for your support and encouragement yesterday. I feel a deeper love for you because of your courage. I guess the reason it is so difficult to define love is that it is an accumulation of so many gifts of your selflessness that it blends into a warmth that holds us together. I am beginning to learn to accept your gifts and will treasure them forever."

CHAPTER 4

ANOTHER CHANCE

Several years later, I would confront this criminal again, unexpectedly. I began my morning routine by tuning our bedroom television to the morning newscast while getting ready for work. I was still lying in bed when a picture of the rapist priest flashed on the screen. Initial shock blocked my mind from absorbing the details of the news accompanying the pictures. But soon I realized that the news was about an automobile accident in the Scranton Wilkes-Barre area involving two priests, one of whom had died, the other survived after having been trapped and ultimately freed from the car. In a later broadcast, I learned that it was the rapist who had survived.

My mind was reeling for days, focused on the news. The similarities of the accident including the same location of Fred's fatal auto accident, led to the possible conclusion that by some freak mystery of chance, justice had been served. I was possessed by a strong need to determine the facts of the accident and compare them to those of my first husband's fatality. Fortunately, a friend agreed to travel by my side on a journey to solve my unanswered questions.

During the two hour drive, my mind raced to formulate a plan. Our first stop was the local newspaper *The Times Leader's*

archives. I bought a detailed area map because as I read the newspaper account of the priest's accident, I wanted to be able to pinpoint the exact site of the crash. The other half of the mystery was knowing exactly where Fred's crash had been. I never considered that detail important before but since there was a possibility that the location of the two crashes in someway coincided, I continued exploring the newspaper records. And there it was. On the microfilm screen for February 8, 1965, was Fred's crushed white Ford Convertible along with front page headlines. In the cold dreary room filled with steel cabinets of news history, I suddenly felt flushed.

Shock and relief surfaced simultaneously as I stared at the picture of crumbled and flattened metal from my past. The image rushed forward. My friend held my body from collapse until the waves of emotion passed and my legs felt solid again. This report, complete with photograph, had appeared in the area paper where the accident happened but had not been printed in my local paper where the only account of the tragedy was Fred's obituary along with his graduation picture.

As I read through the details of both accidents, I referred to the map, certain that both happened in the same place. As I located the exact site of Fred's fatality, I realized that the two crashes occurred directly across the Susquehanna River from each other. It was as if the water mirrored the two, reflecting good and evil on opposite banks of the river. Two issues surfaced as I stood there in that room of newspaper archives. First, I needed another confrontation with my rapist which I resolved to pursue immediately. Second, my frozen grief was beginning to thaw and my need to mourn Fred's death surfaced.

My companion and I left the newspaper office and placed several calls in an attempt to locate the injured priest. Luckily, I learned that he was receiving treatment at a public rehabilitation center rather than within the protective walls of a Catholic sanctuary. We were able to walk into the medical building without interference. After discovering his empty private room, we were directed to a large gymnasium where many patients were involved in physical therapy. A staff member directed the two of us to a corner of the room where he was; I spotted a vaguely familiar man strapped into an upright wheelchair. As I approached the crouched body, the face that lifted was indeed the remains of my rapist. I introduced myself. He recognized me but any ounce of compassion I felt for his injured body vanished when he referred to me as "Romie". That friendly nickname originated when he instructed me in Catholic doctrine before my conversion and marriage to Fred. He destroyed the privileged trust with the rape and would never again deserve my respect.

Although my mind had been on a high speed chase for justice that day, I began by asking him about his own accident. He launched into a detailed account of his traumatic experience. As I listened, I felt a renewed anger seething inside. The moment arrived as he told about being trapped inside the car. I erupted with rage.

"Now you know exactly how I felt when you trapped and raped me!" my voice echoed throughout the gymnasium and several staff members rushed to the aid of their patient-priest. The tone of my voice must have sounded threatening. His raised arm signaled them to stop and he continued to listen as I began to piece together my theories. I was sure this car crash was much more than mere coincidence. This was revenge and justice for the violent damage that he had inflicted on Fred's wife, initiated by a higher power than either of us. I accused him of somehow, I had no idea how, being involved in Fred's death. My mind raced from one possibility to another. This man and Fred knew each other very well. Perhaps he convinced Fred to meet him in that distant community. Maybe Fred was carrying out some unsuspecting plan for this priest. I spat out one accusation after another. The frail figure strapped to the chair was speechless and his head drooped even lower. I demanded again that he look me in the eye as he mumbled denials. My fiery eyes met his and searched his soul, he was visibly shaken with fear. I had had enough but warned him of my return if any further details of Fred's death implicated him. As my friend and I left, the fire of rage burned through every muscle in my body. I was determined to follow my instincts and learn every detail of my first husband's death.

Unfortunately, over the next several weeks, my determination was repeatedly thwarted by destroyed police and hospital records. I even investigated possible eyewitnesses and police officers who might have recalled the tragedy. Several return trips to that vicinity proved fruitless. Although everyone I spoke to was sympathetic, none could provide helpful details, so I was left with only intuition. However, when I contacted the mortuary where Fred's body had been prepared for burial, the son of the owner now managed the business. He agreed to speak to his retired father and search old records for information. The younger man suggested that I stop by and pick up any available records.

As I crossed the threshold of the Crouse's Funeral Home, I felt that someone had reset the clock to February 1965. A windstorm of emotions weakened my knees and heightened my senses. As I steadied myself, the long corridor was suddenly lined with floral tributes and sympathy baskets of flowers. Colors everywhere splashed against the stark white walls. My eye followed the line of flowers into the large room at the end of the hall. As I traced the unsteady steps of a young widow, hushed voices and organ music surrounded me. A heavy weight seemed to pull my heart from its usual place down to my stomach. I squared my shoulders. I was standing before a marble coffin. My arms began to ache as my mind's eye gazed into the still face and body dressed in his wedding suit. His arms would never hold me again; my arms never had the chance to hold him and say goodbye. A few silent tears then back to reality as I blinked to clear my vision. Goodbye Fred.

CHAPTER 5

MYSTERY UNRAVELED

Much to my surprise, another opportunity for healing came unexpectedly during a psychodrama training several years later. Soon after I established my counseling practice, my interest in psychodrama had been fostered by an occasional meeting with another therapist who specialized in the techniques of action therapy. Nancy's personal warmth and her unassuming nature allowed me to risk a professional relationship with her. When she offered a series of monthly training days, I participated in them for several months. Her training method involved the practical applications of psychodrama, focusing each program on a general human experience such as emotional stalling, spirituality or losses.

Those of us attending the training were invited to participate in an enactment each week. This method of learning had been effective. This action model for therapeutic healing had application for a variety of counseling methods like "empty chair" technique. As my trust in small groups steadily grew, I even willingly took part in these psychodrama scenes. Then one Saturday as I entered the training room, I thought, "Today I will observe the action from a detached position." I had been exhausted from a demanding work week and a long list of household duties awaited after the three hour training. My resolve was firm as I greeted other trainees, several familiar participants and two new women.

Nancy warmed up the group by discussing the program purpose and made introductions. The next exercise in our beginning segment involved selecting a position in the room which each of us felt represented our attitude toward the training. I perched on a window ledge in the far corner of the room to signify my observer role for this session. One of the newcomers sat along the wall near my position. As I watched and listened to this young woman explain her desire to "just observe" the training, something quite unfamiliar began happening.

Uncontrollable vibrations started in my stomach, moved up into my chest and arms, then moved down into my legs. When this young woman said that she was twenty-two-years old, I realized she mirrored Mrs. Fred Fischer, the young widow. The fear surfaced after thirty years. I refused to suppress this storm of feelings. In a shaky voice, I asked for Nancy's guidance to face the torrent of fear engulfing my body at that moment. She immediately set the stage by asking where I was and what was happening.

"February 7, 1965, Sunday morning 2 A.M. I am standing in the kitchen with the telephone in my hand. A strange voice inside the phone just told me that my husband had been killed in an automobile accident. I screamed, releasing frozen terror from my throat. DISBELIEF. "It can't be true-someone has made a terrible mistake." ANGER. "How dare they call and wake me up in the middle of the night." CONFUSION. "Where is Fred? He promised to be back by now." URGENCY. "I've got to get dressed! They said he was in a hospital in Wilkes-Barre; that's more than a one hour drive from here. I've got to get to him." Somewhere in the back of my mind a plan began to take shape. Leta, my next door neighbor, could watch our babies. Change clothes, off with nightgown. Grab slacks, sweater, sneakers and socks.

Now, in the safety of a psychodrama group, my body shook from head to toe as I returned to that terrifying night. At that moment, my only thought, my only desire, my singular mission was to reach my beloved's side, hold him in my arms and assure him that he was going to live.

"That night in 1965, my parents arrive soon after Leta had called them. Although I continue to voice my need to be with Fred, my mom reminds me there is nothing I can do in Wilkes-Barre. Fred was gone. "your place is here with the children," she said.

Through the psychodrama experience, I was able to express my long lost true emotions that had been repressed on that traumatic night. Leta had betrayed my trust. I needed her friendship but she chose to call my parents. I didn't want my parents there; I wanted her. "Leta, you were the one person in my life whom I trusted to honor my immediate need and you failed. If only you had believed in yourself as much as I believed in you. But you didn't. Instead you called on others to handle this emergency." I felt relief in confronting Leta to finally express the words that I could not voice before.

"Mom, you always take charge of situations. You are very good in crises because your own alcoholic father created chaos in your life for so long. That night, you refused to listen because of your own desire to take control of yet another crisis. You never put aside your own need to control, giving that power to others, especially your daughter. I needed to go to my husband's side, hold him in my arms before his lifeless body turned cold and say goodbye to him. You closed your heart and mind tightly to that need, to any need, but your own. You failed miserably that night in my darkest hour of need."

"Dad, you stood silently by your wife's side, in the shadow of her control, refusing to challenge her. I know now that you desperately wanted to stand beside me but your own fear of mom's powerful manipulation prevented you from acting on my behalf. I was completely drained of my own strength to move as I fought an internal battle to remain sane. I needed your added strength as an anchor in that storm of death and chaos but you couldn't, you wouldn't, you didn't." Through the power of psychodrama, I finally was achieving a sense of completeness.

The scene changed and I was at the Mercy Hospital Emergency Room. Rushing to Fred's side, my beating heart makes breathing painful. In my mind's eye, my arms reach out. I meet my own desperate longing to hold Fred in my arms as I feel his head on my aching heart and say goodbye to my lover, husband, hero in the way that I needed to in 1965.

Even though decades had elapsed between the tragedy and that moment in a psychodrama training session, my sigh of relief and sense of satisfaction were just as complete. That culmination spanned the gulf and connected one to the other. The flood of emotions washed away the huge expanse of time, joining the two links in the ongoing chain of life's events.

My goal in therapy to remember Fred and my life together had gradually returned. I knew without a doubt that he loved both children. Our marriage may have not been the best but I watched as his joy overflowed when he was with his son and daughter. Yet, my therapy sessions continued to unravel the mystery of lost memories.

After confronting the priest, I felt much more trust with Caroll and openly discussed my dark side. Somewhere in the dark recesses of this whirlwind life, another aspect of my personality had emerged and split apart from the Superwoman. This part was a sexual manipulator who used men whom I picked up, played with and quickly tossed aside. As I glanced back over the life span of this shadow, I saw a pile of discarded male bodies, all faceless strangers.

While I was the Director of Domestic Relations; out of town professional meetings, conventions and seminars became the catalyst for adventures because there my dark side could casually manipulate men in hotel bars while still remaining anonymous. Even if colleagues suspected the game I played, most were male players of the same game or they simply closed their eyes to the behavior.

The seductress's life spanned five years. During that period, that part remained discreet so that my very public professional career was protected and I could continue to care for my thriving family.

As we explored this aspect of my hidden existence, I educated myself about the aftereffects of sexual abuse. Caroll recommended several books on the subject including *The Courage to Heal* written by Ellen Bass and Laura Davis. My daily journaling, too, focused on the past as I wondered why. WHY? When my life was both personally and professionally rewarding would I deliberately sabotage it by risky behavior?

Why couldn't I just fall asleep, recall my past and end this cycle of mystery? I wanted to remember the good and the bad, instead forgetting the negative and always putting a positive spin on every thought, incident and image. For example, I remembered being punished by being isolated in Sarah's house but don't remember what my crime was; I remember Mom sent me to choose a lilac switch, but don't remember my behavior that led up to that punishment. I want to hold onto the past when it comes and yet I feel like I am being tempted with small little windows of things past and it's not enough to complete the puzzle. Have I forgotten my own crime as well as others?

CHAPTER 6

THE DARKER SIDE

Journal Entry:
It was the same monster that had loomed in the shadows of my life and it came at me when I wasn't able to fight. I think I began to try to tame the monster when I chose men outside my marriage to have sex with. There weren't many but I was in control. I chose the man; I chose the time and place, I beat the dragon. There were even occasions that I chose the man, then refused to face the monster and felt satisfied that I could keep the door closed and not let it attack. It was just there begging for my permission. No, I will not relinquish my control. This thing can be weakened.

A vivid dream: I remember reaching for the light beside my bed but when I turned it on, sparks flew out everywhere. I struggled to turn it off but the sparks won't stop. I finally crawled on the floor and pulled the plug to stop the sparks. Does this mean that I am afraid that my journey to recover my past is dangerous? Am I afraid that somehow everything will go haywire? I am afraid that my life will get out of control. I've been so good at keeping my emotions under control. So controlled that I don't even know feelings anymore. I realize what an expert I've become at controlling myself that now that I've begun to explore old violations, I'm afraid of going out of control. I feel like just raging forever. I want to release myself from all the covered up anger and pain that I have so neatly tucked away. Yet, I am afraid that, like the electric light, I will become just so many sparks of energy out of control.

As I continued weekly therapy sessions, I found that when my thoughts were focused on my past, I was able to write them down easier than I could speak about them. Between counseling, I continued keeping a journal. After nearly 24 months of therapy, several journals were filled with thoughts on paper. Early morning had always been my time of quiet before my demanding schedule began. Often the words flowed so easily on the page that I was surprised at the results. It was as if my pen and subconscious were connected. Thoughts weren't always first before I wrote; the words occasionally jumped out from the page.

Entry: *Good morning god; the quiet sounds of morning calm my soul. My body aches but my soul is free to reach beyond my physical limitations. I rejoice in the struggle; I know the climb is difficult but the rewards are marvelous. The agony is nothing in comparison. Teach me to take the right steps. Life is meant to be difficult often so that we can learn to touch the spiritual world around us. Come walk with me and I will never slip in my walk through the lessons of life.*

My letters to God day after day were full of my search for happiness. I longed for peace. My longing became stronger as the whirlpool of memories began to gain momentum. It was an inner struggle between the happiness I had always believed in and the pain and anger that was building up just below the surface of my mind.

Good morning God, the pressure of yesterday spills over into the morning. It makes it difficult to clear my mind for today's talk with you. The shadows of night still linger like some of the darkness in my life. Come to my rescue before I drown in self pity. Lift my spirits like you lift the shadows and replace them with the light of morning.

Through these writings, more memories began to surface and in the safety of Caroll's office, I began to clearly remember and talk about them.

I was twelve-years-old when my best friend Barb and I began bike rides around town, roller skating on Saturday afternoons and meeting boys on our adventures. Remember James Dean? He was my teenage idol. Lots of guys at the skating rink dressed like him. You know, blue jeans and white T-shirts with rolled-up sleeves, a pack of cigarettes tucked in one sleeve, showing off bulging arm muscles. The memory of being twelve and those freedom rides began to emerge.

One afternoon, we were racing back to Barb's house after skating when one of the "James Deans" called to us. He was standing near the bushes in Way's Garden, our short cut. I could hardly believe my ears. He knew my name, Barb's, too. He motioned for us to come over and talk to him. He must have been sixteen or seventeen. I was thrilled and went right to him. I vaguely heard Barb's voice. She was saying something about being afraid because she might be late getting home. Nothing mattered except being with my James Dean idol. The two of us talked for awhile. He said I was pretty and he loved my ponytail as he ran his fingers through my long hair. As he talked, he took my hand and we walked into the secluded part of the park. I was so excited I hardly noticed that his hold was stronger as he whispered words of passion that made my heart pound in my ears.

Then I did notice something was wrong. He was unbuttoning my blouse with one hand and fumbling with my shorts with the other. His lips crushed against mine. Barb was running now and I wanted her to come back. His sweaty body engulfed mine. When I looked into his eyes, something scary was there. A stare, a faraway blank stare, filled his beautiful blue-grey eyes. Then he pushed me to the ground, pulled my shorts and panties down around my ankles, unzipped his jeans and forced himself into me. I felt a sharp pain before everything went blank except the dark clouds above and the gritty gravel underneath. I closed my eyes and faded into the dirt. The scream of terror stuck in my throat as I fell deeper into the darkness. Then he was standing up, brushing off dirt from his clothes, zipping up his jeans. He walked away without another word. I lay there among the grime and bushes, lost in a faraway blank stare.

"Caroll, do you think that had anything to do with the way my life changed when I was twelve? This is really tough talking about, Caroll. Being violated. This is embarrassing. If only I would have stayed with Barb. I didn't even scream or fight back. What was the matter with me? My mom was right when she called me a bad kid. I guess I deserved what happened in Way's Garden," I said.

Caroll's remarks began to alter my view of the incident, as she explained that no one deserves to be raped, "The violator was stronger and taller than you. He used the element of surprise to overpower you; you did nothing to be ashamed of."

The shame I felt of sexual manipulations of adult males lifted as I acknowledged being raped at the age of twelve in the park. Caroll suggested that the trauma of rape produced this dark side of my life to balance the out-of-control feelings of being assaulted when I was a teenager.

The morning after one of my sessions with Caroll I woke feeling very on edge. My skin was crawling and I felt scared. I realized that I was having a flashback of my rape experience. I felt panic and fear. I was fighting but didn't cry out or scream for help. I realized my hands were clutched in fists, my arms ached from the intensity of my tightly held fists. Even several minutes after I was fully awake, when I went to the bathroom, I was holding on to my panties. I felt I wanted to pull them up to resist what my abductor was trying to do to pull them down. I tried to stay with my feelings but was afraid to give them a voice without guidance. I called Caroll. She scheduled a session for the next day.

I kept very busy in the twenty four hour before my session; I fixed our family's evening meal then went right to bed. I found myself using sleep as a safe haven. Although there were nights when sleep allowed past experiences to reach my consciousness or opened the door to new dimensions, I couldn't always remember the messages but I was sure that I was in contact with those experiences that helped me continue the healing that had begun.

During several counseling sessions, I revisited Way's Garden. The power of suppressed fury was almost too frightening to bear as wave after wave of magnified anger stormed within the safety of Caroll's counseling office. Afterward, the tone of emotions turned from red to blue as I grieved the loss of a healthy adolescence.

I realized that my guilt caused many reactions then. I thought that if my mother found out about the rape, she would blame me. She would have said "you should not have been roller skating with that crowd of boys. You should have stayed home instead". I knew then that I would be punished for doing something wrong.

As I remembered, I understood why I turned away from childhood friends. I knew then that the reason I rejected them and turned instead to the street gangs from the "other side of the tracks". After the rape, I felt dirty; I couldn't face my friends. The scars of rape left an image both unattractive and ashamed. I believed that I was no longer worthy of their friendships. I was soiled inside and outside. Even bathing didn't take away the dirty feeling I carried inside from my rape in the park.

After years of self destructive behavior, on December 31, 1999 at the stroke of midnight, I ended an addiction to nicotine. The connection between the start of my smoking habit at twelve and the rape became painfully clear. Although I was well into recovery and healthy living, it took additional strategies to become a nonsmoker.

I had no desire to confront the teenager who stole my innocence. I was just relieved to understand the impact and forgave myself for sexually manipulating men with no faces. However, the dark side of my personality was not yet willing to accept this new understanding. My commitment after one of my sessions with Caroll: "I want to learn to love each part of who I am and together as I bring that intimacy into my awareness, I will be able to love in a new way and a new day." The many parts were coming together for strength and encouragement to walk the path I had begun. I knew the first steps would be difficult but I did not turn away. I was committed to my journey and refused to allow walls to stand in my way. Those walls could be removed, brick by brick if necessary, but I removed them with new determination. I wanted to accept myself and learn to define my life instead of others defining me.

CHAPTER 7

MIRROR IMAGE
TRANSFORMED

During my ongoing therapy, the previously delayed executive director training at the YWCA's National Headquarters in Arizona was scheduled. This time I was obligated to attend. I enjoyed the stimulation of workshops and relaxing evenings.

Throughout the two weeks, three other directors and I spent our evening meal together, then returned to our hotel rooms to study the training materials for the upcoming workshops. One particular evening after dinner, someone suggested that we stop at the hotel bar for a few drinks. After attempting conversation over loud music, one of the women threw up her hands in frustration and suggested that we join the crowd on the dance floor. The glass of wine had warmed my veins and loosened my tense muscles and I began to enjoy the music. We found a small spot on the dance floor, formed a circle and started swaying with the rhythm. As I danced, I noticed my reflection in a nearby full length mirrored wall.

As one song faded into another without pause, my companions seemed to disappear, leaving only my reflection and myself dancing face to face. The reflection's movements became increasingly provocative as I turned and twisted. Then my image moved out of the mirror onto the dance floor. She had a name: the seductress.

My other self moved in closer to a young male seated at the bar. He asked if I was staying at the hotel. She/I invited him to the room. She?I played with him on the short walk from the barroom, through the lobby, past the indoor pool and down the hall to her first floor room. Completely in control, I initiated the embraces, pressing my body tightly against his. Recognizing his readiness, she/I moved closer to the bed.

Afterwards he lay exhausted across the bed but she/I wanted a swim in the lobby pool. Grabbing a white terry bath towel to wrap in she/I headed to the pool. At 2 A.M. the hotel was asleep, only a few soft lights in the hall led to her destination. At that moment, she was aware of a deeper, more significant destiny. There at the pool's edge with the glass ceiling admitting a moonlit, starry sky, she was the center of the universe. Water held so many wonderful memories, like her risky young adult adventure when she met Fred. Water was about to heal a painful past. She stood tall and proud as the warm chlorine mist moved up her legs, swirled around her hips, gently fell on her left breast and scarred right, caressed her shoulders, encircled her arms and hands, penetrated her face and soft curls until she breathed a gulp of air before stepping into the warm water. I was aware that her existence was coming to an end. My therapy sessions revealed the long held secrets that had created and sustained her. Her shame was gone; her pride restored. Her need to control was over. She exited as she entered. The water birthed her; this water was a final transformation. As I slowly returned to the water's surface, I felt a slight chill ripple through my body. A quick glance around restored reality.

To all the faceless men who became players on this seductress's stage, I send heartfelt regrets. You were outlets for my anger and revenge, uninformed victims, ignorant as I was of the deep darkness created by sexual abuse and rape.

One of the bricks that I was determined to remove from that solid wall was my fear of intimacy with Paul. I planned a get away weekend for us to celebrate our 23rd anniversary. Detailing aspects of playful sex, I was filled with hope of achieving a healthy and exciting physical intimacy between us. Small steps throughout the evening-a romantic dinner, champagne drinks in our hotel room, then slow safe touches to stimulate our arousal. Paul's patience and gentleness gradually created a safe haven; I let myself experience a natural flow of lovemaking. Afterwards, the room's whirlpool tub filled with mounds of bubble bath surrounded two lovers in each other's arms. An important moment in this journey through recovery. Once again water provided an opportunity for change.

My handwritten anniversary card to Paul:

The gifts of yourself are the best gifts of all and the most difficult to accept. I know I have to work harder at accepting and giving but please, don't stop giving and loving; it is what has made the difference for us as a couple. I know I love you today more than yesterday and we will grow. Loveya, Rosemary.

CHAPTER 8

STEP BY STEP TOWARD CELEBRATION

There were two separate occasions in my recovery from the rape trauma in Way's Garden. The first was unplanned; occurring during an intense group therapy session that I agreed to co-facilitate with my Lincoln University companion, Chuck. This particular session, I was helping a young man express his repressed childhood anger. I was kneeling across from him with a stack of square floor pillows between us. Slamming his tight fists into those foam pillows, his rage surfaced with stormy words of hatred. My role was to validate his anger, to remain calm through his expressions and to encourage him to release his emotions in this healthy manner instead of physically abusing his loved ones. Something unexpected happened as I made eye contact with this client. A small ache began to grow in my stomach until it jabbed at my right side. My arms stiffened in fear and I felt my back arch in a defensive posture. The face opposite was transformed into that young James Dean look-a-like from Way's Garden.

I managed to mask my inner turmoil until I could discuss it privately with my trusted friend. Within twenty four hour, sitting in Chuck's office, his guided imagery opened up the space for honoring my feelings. As I traveled back to the scene of my rape, I felt the terror of being forced down into the dirt, felt the pain of the pebbles on my back, my shoulders pushed harder and harder into the gravel and stones. Then the body above stole the sunlight from view as he violated me. A series of sensations began at my left ankle, moved up through both legs and hips, traveled through my upper body before settling as heavy lumps in my throat. Struggling to breathe and free this blockage, I used the power of visualization to create a pure white dove who willingly attached itself to the string of heavy lumps, stone-frozen fear, in my throat and flew upward into the now sunlit sky. The stones, the frozen fear from being raped decades ago, moved freely through and out of my body until they were released into the universe. This technique of guided imagery, useful in psychodrama training, became the key to releasing those frozen feelings trapped in my body that were decades old.

Another step in my recovery from his sexual violation in Way's Garden came later for closure and celebration. After attending a women's conference workshop on rituals, I began to consider a personal ceremony to acknowledge the transition I had undergone between age twelve and fifty-two-years old. By 1994, I had been in a private counseling practice for five years.

Rituals had often marked special events in my life: baptisms, confirmations, weddings and funerals. Each one had been planned with special attention to important details. Although no longer affiliated with religious hierarchies, I continued to foster spirituality within my being. Throughout the months of planning for this special event, a growing sense of sacredness evolved within the theme of this ritual. My attention focused on symbols to represent a transition from powerlessness to empowerment. As my personal healing journey had transformed victim to survivor to victor, this ritual represented victory.

The ritual became an important gift to my self-worth by honoring my discovery journey. I chose symbolic clothes, music and witnesses as carefully as I had for my wedding day. The exact date became clear when the local rape counseling center announced an evening vigil commemorating the power of women entitled "Take Back the Night." I immediately knew this was the appropriate date for my celebration.

Paul and I had arrived early in advance of the 5 P.M. start of the ritual. Way's Garden was alive with families and groups of people scattered throughout the park benches and walkways. One group of young males was laughing and playing loud music on their boom box. How was I ever going to create a sacred reverence? A passing thought, "I'll just ask them to turn off the music." Followed by my own silent response, "No, they won't understand." At that moment, several invited guests arrived and my attention shifted to greeting them. Each of my eight invited guests whom I had shared my story understood my journey and agreed to attend this important ritual. As Paul stood by my side, I welcomed them to the park.

The ritual began when I asked my friends to form a circle in a grassy spot near the rear of the park, "Join me now to stand on the spot where a violent crime was committed against an innocent twelve year-old woman child in the summer of 1957."

As I quietly spoke of that long ago summer day, I noticed a solemn hush settling into the immediate area. The young males had turned off their music, a mother and two toddlers sitting on a nearby park bench moved closer together. Several other couples on the walkway slowed their walk and held hands. I sensed a respectful hush.

"Safe and sound, yes, but isolated from the pain and fear. The steel vest and the shame of sexual violation left me distant and unworthy of friendship and love," The details of that faraway moment flowed from my lips. My head was covered in a black veil and I wore a metallic turtleneck sweater to represent my protective armor.

Then I left the circle to walk the few steps alone to those bushes, the scene of the crime. I lit a vigil candle to honor myself as a young twelve- year-old girl while the music and haunting lyrics of my selected song *"Child Inside My Soul"* played on a portable tape machine. *"...there is a child inside my soul, she's calling me. I cannot leave her for I know her well. I won't deceive her, for her story I'll tell..."* I invited my guests to walk to the center of the park where I shed my black veil and metal shirt. Under the shirt was the same pink dress that I had worn when confronting the priest. This pink dress represented my personal power of victory.

As I spoke of a transformation from victim to survivor, I invited each witness to briefly hold a new garment, a white shawl of softly woven yarn. I then wrapped the chosen shawl around my shoulders to represent a new willingness to receive their affection. I planted a white rose bush in the heart of the park while talking about its purpose, "Her thorns protect the white buds and blooms from perpetrators who might attempt to arrest her growth. She stands in the open park, never overshadowed by large trees, her roots reaching deep into the nourishing soil, unobstructed by wandering, selfish, larger roots. Her space is dedicated to nourishing her."

In closing the ceremony, I joined the circle of loving energy and silently asked for healing power to be sent to other survivors in the universe. While I thanked my guests, handing a white rose to each, the most unexpected moment happened. A young female, most likely twelve-years-old, appeared seemingly from nowhere and joined hands with my friends to receive a rose, too. Her presence affirmed the value of the sacred ritual.

With the layers of shame lifted , past events began to make sense. I was amazed at the capacity of the unconscious to avoid dealing the emotional trauma of being raped! One particular revelation astonished me when I realized how carefully I created distance from my own daughters. When each turned twelve, I enrolled in college and drowned myself in academic learning, thereby running away from any reminder of that painful rape incident.

Audrey Lorde writes in *"Sister Outsider"* that *"this cruelty between us, this harshness, is a piece of the legacy of hate with which we were inoculated from the time we were born by those who intended it to be an injection of death. But we adapted, learned to take it in and use it, unscrutinized. Yet at what cost! In order to withstand the weather, we had to become stone and now we bruise ourselves upon the other who is closest."*

Much later I walked past the park. It was dark but the park was dotted with drops of white light. I glanced at the spot where I was raped. The deep foliage that hid my young body and my rapist were gone. In its place, tall bushes stood with wide open spaces between them. No one can bury a young girl's soul and steal her womanness in this airy, open space.

CHAPTER 9

REFLECTIONS

One afternoon therapy session, I rushed into Caroll's office to tell her breathlessly about the Sunday evening vision of a kewpie doll. The mysterious incident flooded my senses because the only kewpie doll I could remember belonged to dad's mother, Grandma Cummings. Why then would the doll memory be connected with such terrifying feelings? There was definitely something wrong with the connection. I became intent on unraveling this mystery with Caroll's help.

Between sessions, I explored photo albums trying to connect these foreign feelings to unravel the mystery. Whenever my eyes scanned Grandpa's face another bolt jolted through my body. A photo of grandfather and me caught my attention. The snapshot was taken in the snowy backyard of my parents' home. I wore matching toddler leggings and coat. He was holding me, a two-year-old, in his arms but my position was most revealing; I was pulled as far away from him as possible, not normally a young granddaughter's response to being held by a loving grandfather. Neither one of us was smiling for the camera.

The most vivid part of my dream was being in a musty old living room and hearing heavy breathing. Someone held me on his lap in that living room. I

felt my center tighten. Was it his penis hard that I felt close to my crotch while he held me? Why did you scare me so? Didn't you know I trusted you? My daddy wasn't there to protect me.

Then I had a sense of a cellar door that I was trying to close but there was a monster-a blob-forcing it open; even oozing out around the edges of the door. I didn't have enough strength to force the door closed.

The confusion became even more intense when I approached my parents for answers about Dad's patriarch. Dad talked about a hard working father while mom spoke gently about her kind father-in-law. During one evening's table talk with my parents, the conversation started to get really emotional when I said something about God being a woman. She said "You're wrong and by the way, lately you've been different. You seem to abandon everything you were taught."

I knew I'd struck a cord to challenge her religious beliefs.

"So mom, what about the equality of the sexes?"

She replied, "One always has to love more; I support my husband in everyway."

I guess I was setting the stage for revealing my secrets when next I asked her, "Do you want to hear what happened when I was twelve?"

A firm reply, "No. Everybody has things that their parents don't know about."

I thought, *"Well, that subject is closed."*

I approached another subject: "My earliest memory was when I was in a high chair in a small hallway."

"Yes," she replied, "I often put you there when you were bad. You cried for awhile and no one did come until you quieted down." That was confirmation of my vivid memory and the fearful isolation.

While mom was forthcoming, I decided to continue, "Mom, describe my grandparents' bedroom. Help me remember."

When she started to describe the room, she mentioned that that was where the kewpie doll was. My reaction was instant. My whole body literally shook from head to toe. I fought against the tremors for a minute then asked, "Why did you mention the doll?" She remembered that I asked her about the doll before.

Mom was curious, "Why is the doll so important?"

I said," I have a feeling that something happened in that bedroom. Mom, why don't I remember grandpa with fondness?"

"He wasn't affectionate. He never even showed affection toward your grandma." *Here comes the justification,* I thought. Her answer, "There were no girls."

I noticed that when Mom and I were talking, Dad sat silently. I wondered, *"Dad, what are you thinking? Why aren't you talking?"*

Mom promised to let me know if she remembered any more details about my grandfather. I thanked her for being willing to help.

I said, "I hope now you understand why I have acted different lately. I'm preoccupied with trying to fill in some blank spaces in my past."

Her response, "There is a ten year period in my life that is blank but I accept the fact of lost years."

I said, "I can't accept that for myself and am focused on retrieving those memories."

I felt that mom and I bridged a gap that evening. Even though she refused to hear about my rape at twelve, she was willing to listen and respond with other useful information.

⊰◈⊱

Monday morning when I got up my legs ached. By afternoon, I left work early with an unbearable headache. My body's response to the mention of the kewpie doll was scary. I wanted to try to place myself in my grandparents' bedroom. I knew Paul questioned the validity of my memories; sometimes I did, too. *"Did they really happen? Or am I trying so hard to remember that I create the incidents?"* He planted a seed of doubt in my mind.

Plant a seed – my body reacts – Why? Planting a seed has to do with intercourse; a man plants his seed in a woman. Oh, I had plenty of seeds planted. Planting a seed happens in a garden, too. My grandfather had a garden. I do remember going out in the summer and eating a tomato right off the vine. He was there.

CHAPTER 10

TEACHER AND STUDENT

Since Dad's three brothers were deceased and only one of his sisters-in-law was still living, my questions were directed to her, my Aunt Thelma. Our conversation was unforgettable.

A remarkable eighty-year-old woman greeted me with enthusiasm at her apartment door. She welcomed my spontaneous visit as eagerly as Sarah used to whenever I interrupted her daily routine. Aunt Thelma's well-groomed stout figure stood surprisingly majestic after physical sacrifices and hard work during the Great Depression, World War II era and her own parents' aging dependency. She now chose a solitary life of independence. Much like my Nana, Thelma's husband's death signaled an internal mechanism of self sufficiency.

While we exchanged casual conversation that evening, I reflected on her life. As a young bride, she and her husband, Uncle Paul, lived on the Cummings' farm. She, of all the daughters-in-law, had an opportunity to become intimately acquainted with my grandparents. Eventually she and my Uncle Paul and their son moved near my parents for employment in a war related manufacturing plant. I understood that Uncle Paul had been attentive to Mom while my dad was fighting World War II.

I remembered the year of major loss for our family which certainly must have been felt most acutely by this gentle woman sitting across the room. That year, 1960, her husband, her mother-in-law, and her father-in-law died within the span of thirteen months. My grandmother had been diagnosed with uterine cancer. While everyone's prayers and concerns focused on Grandma's failing health, her husband suddenly died of a heart attack. After his death, Grandma let go of life within three months to follow him.

Just months after burying both parents, Uncle Paul died of a massive heart attack. Throughout the months of mourning, I do remember one fortress of strength and compassion, Aunt Thelma. Later in my life, she became another role model as I dealt with my own husband's death. This night, though, I sought her guidance with another turmoil, this mysterious grandfather image.

As I gingerly approached the main purpose of my visit, her body language remained as welcoming as usual. Relaxed in her armchair, her legs propped on a cushioned stool , her undivided attention focused on our conversation.

"Aunt Thelma, I think Grandpa did something awful to me when I was a child," I said. I held my breath as those terrifying words flashed like neon lights on the four walls of her tiny apartment.

She frowned slightly and replied, "I am not surprised." She continued, "Although he never crossed sexual boundaries with me, I heard rumors about his sexual advances toward a school teacher. When Grandma was hospitalized, he had forced unwelcome sexual contacts onto a young visiting teacher."

I explained my dilemma with vague memories and conflicting feelings. "I thought that he violated me, but didn't he love me? How could this be?"

Aunt Thelma and I talked openly about family intimacy. She commented on the obvious lack of physical contact between her in-laws. We both remembered how shocked we all were when my grandparents publicly kissed each other during their fiftieth wedding anniversary celebration. My grandparents were rarely in the same room together, let alone embracing or kissing. Aunt Thelma continued to share with me her insights about this couple whom she observed from her adult viewpoint.

As we talked that evening, my imaginary grandfather gradually became replaced by the reality of a husband, father-in-law and adult male. Her words flowed like water washing away cobwebs and dust from my own buried vision. She spoke of her mother-in-law's kindnesses; Thelma learned the ways of managing a household from Mary. Mary was the one who stayed by her side during the hours of giving birth at the farm house.

She recounted, "As for Arthur, my father-in-law, he was rarely inside except to eat and sleep. He was either in the fields or busy with church business or other activities in town. Your grandfather ordered his sons to tend the farm chores but he seldom had a playful moment; there seemed to always be a chill in that farmhouse and I was happy when Paul announced our move to the factory town."

Here two adult women sat in quiet reflection of a shared story: she, the teacher, I, the student. Then her voice suddenly became hushed and her eyes clouded over with mist. She said "I understand your pain because I too had been violated as a child."

Her words, "I was molested," initially shocked me as they flowed from her deepest secret recesses of her memory. She said that she never told anyone before my visit. She was four and living on her parents' farm. During harvest, her job was carrying water buckets into the fields for the migrant workers.

As she walked through the tall cornfields between the barn and the distant wheat fields, a male field hand viciously attacked and molested her. As her hushed tones of this crime surrounded us, I envisioned a four-year-old being overpowered by a giant, sweaty male body forcing her to the ground with water pails tumbling out of sight, stripped of her innocence and clothing and left to recover the empty pails.

In the span of moments, Aunt Thelma and I bridged a chasm of womanhood as we joined hearts in the common bond of survivors. When we embraced in farewell, my heart overflowed with gratitude. Maybe I was not crazy because of the seemingly reconcilable feelings I was experiencing about my father's father; I no longer felt isolated.

CHAPTER 11

FORESHADOWS

My strength and courage were becoming increasingly important values and I was beginning to acknowledge that I was truly worthwhile.

I had a conversation with Paul on his birthday. He wanted to know what was wrong with our relationship? Didn't I know that he would want sex? Was there something about him that I hadn't dealt with that was keeping me from him? Couldn't I separate my past from my present? And on and on.

I told him there was nothing about him that was repulsive. In fact, his love and commitment to our marriage had been the solid foundation that made my recovery possible. The struggle to be sexually vulnerable was still within me; it was not a rejection of him. I tried to explain as best as I could that I was becoming a whole person with a past, present and future. The mending of old wounds was painfully slow; but if he wanted the old me without a past, without feelings, without commitments and understandings, that woman was gone forever.

The next day, I kept my distance from Paul. There was little conversation. An echo in my mind said, *"if you can't say something nice, don't say anything at all."* What does that mean? Was that another reason for not telling of my childhood abuse? Yes, of course! I would have been scolded for saying such awful things. My silence-the sound of silence- rings out so clear now. I couldn't speak for so many reasons. I couldn't jeopardize my special place. I couldn't be responsible for my grandparent's separation. I couldn't speak; I knew it wasn't nice-"Say nothing at all." So many messages. A child's conclusion: it will go away and everything will be fine.

A dream that week:

I was an adult getting ready for a bath but there were many interruptions. First, I had just filled the tub and four people—two women and two men—came in to take a shower. I refused since it took so long to fill the tub. Then when I went to get in, there were four or five women in my tub. I was upset but sat and talked to them. Then out of an attic door in the bathroom, naked men wearing black knit masks came out of the door and everyone was running around confused. Then I finally was getting in the tub and there was a man in a full suit laying deep in the water. He said he loved me and rose to hold me. I let him but said any man who takes his briefcase in the tub with him couldn't love me.

But several weeks later, a bathtub and a mirror led to a major breakthrough in my craziness.

CHAPTER 12

A CHILD'S VOICE

My daily morning routine had included a steaming hot bath. I would fill our old fashion deep bathtub to the brim, slip down into its warmth and wash away overnight and early morning tension. This particular morning was no different from any other until I stood up to step out of the tub. At that moment, the medicine cabinet mirror across from the tub caught my reflection and I came face to face with an overwhelming flood of emotions. As I stood naked and shivering, a nightmare of ghostly fear emerged. "I want my daddy" was the childlike sound that erupted from my throat which had been stuck there for over one-half century.

Paul gently wrapped my body in terrycloth and guided my trembling body out of the bathroom, through the hallway, into the safety of our bedroom. He held me close to his warm body until my own gradually regained stability and I was breathing again. Did I want him to telephone my dad and ask him to come as soon as possible? "Yes, I need my daddy," I said.

When he and mom arrived, I was curled into a tight ball against the bed pillows, holding my emotions in check. Paul directed Mom to stand back while he guided Dad to our bedroom. The sight of him brought some relief as I reached out for his arms. He immediately responded as I sobbed uncontrollably.

After releasing deep, painful grief, I told him about the monsters in the attic and how afraid I had felt without him when he was a soldier. Dad very seldom spoke but that morning he said that I was always his little girl. I had longed to hear these loving, protective words from the most important man in my young life. Now, as I was cradled in his strong arms, I was finally safe to express painful and frightening feelings. The reality of a monster grandfather emerged; I REMEMBERED THE TRAUMA. I was two-years-old.

CHAPTER 13

THE TERROR

The image of a kewpie doll's plump naked body, tiny angel wings and angelic smile appeared as the visual memories surfaced in my bedroom.

The account of being sexually attacked finally flowed freely. Some of the words sounded like a small child's voice while periodically my adult voice told the story. No longer bits and pieces of a puzzle, I told the story in its entirety.

It was the summer, 1944. Mom had volunteered to nurse her mother-in-law back to health after her major surgery. I remember I played outside with neighborhood kids, explored the nooks and crannies of kitchen cupboards, played with toys near the living room bay window and investigated new rooms behind closed doors. "Rosemary, come here right now!" Mom's voice echoes from my memory.

This particular sunny afternoon, my grandfather was recruited to bathe me before dinner. I remember playing outside in a colorful sun suit before Mom's voice called. I loved the cool feeling of splashing in the big tub upstairs at my grandparents' house. So when grandpa lifted me up in his arms for a bath, I giggled with excitement. The story that was unfolding was like looking at a Norman Rockwell portrait of an aging grandfather carrying his toddler granddaughter in his bulky arms up the narrow stairs to the second floor bathroom.

The bright afternoon sunlight reflects off the white bathroom walls. Arthur moves around checking the bathwater filling the tub, gathering towels and unbuttoning my sun suit. Splashes and laughter blend into a sweet melody of innocence as I make sounds while I'm in the tub.

Suddenly, as I recall the sequence of events, I am feeling scared and find it hard to breathe. The little girl's splashes stop. The only sound I hear is his voice saying, "If you tell anyone, I will let the monsters out of the attic." I hear faint drips of water as Arthur lifts me from the tub. I realize that my grandfather wraps a towel around my body, carries me into a bedroom, lays me on his bed and unfolds the towel. I look away from him as he touches my soft folds between my legs. While this grotesque scene unfolds, I only see a kewpie doll on a nearby bedroom dresser to escape the reality.

My father held me in the safety of his arms while I remembered. When finished, he said that if he would have known what happened, he would have protected me. He said that I was always his little girl.

Then he went on to say the words I refused to accept, "Now, put this behind you and get on with your life"

Get on with my life? "No Dad. I cannot push this violence back into my subconscious and pretend it never happened. I know so much more about myself and from now on, I will continue to heal from this terror."

This young childhood incident was the beginning of repressed memories when confusion and fear were too overwhelming for a two-year-old to deal with. Through my process of discovery, I have come to understand the human spirit's ability to use a multitude of coping methods to survive. Both emotional numbness and repression, along with dissociation, were the skills that I used to survive: "*a primary mechanism for inhibiting access to memory*" (Courtois, 1999).

As my memory of that trauma surfaced, I remembered an innocent rescue from a local soldier returning from war. Mom's story of his visit made an important contribution. When Norman stopped at my grandparent's house, I apparently ran to his side as soon as he walked in the front door. He was dressed in his military uniform and Mom suggested that he resembled my dad. I clung to him until he decided that I could tag along while he visited other neighbors during the afternoon. I believe that his visit was soon after I was molested. *Thank you, Norman.*

The idea of my grandparents separating if I told my story was probably one of my early fears and one reason for forgetting my grandfather's abuse for so long; a child's awareness of family matters is wider in scope than adults realize. That was too great a responsibility to take on when I was very young. Also, at two years old, finding words to name what happened were impossible except knowing that what he did was wrong.

When you are small, you trust and love the world. When that trust and love comes crashing down around you, you are destroyed and lay among the rubble. When you look up from the heap, all you see is the destruction around you at first. Finally, you search long and hard and see a ray of light and stare into the light until you have blocked out all the darkness and devastation. Your eye is fixed on the light; it offers hope and healing. You rise up through the dust, blinded by that ray of light. Throughout your journey, the light remains at a distance and you use it as your guide. Nothing else matters except reaching the source of your precious light. You stumble, fall, grope in the darkness but always your eyes focus on that beam of light no matter how faded or distant it becomes. There are others who may block the light with their bodies; resort to holding you in place but you can't allow yourself to stop or look around you. You must keep your focus on the beam of hope. You are hopeful that the light will encircle you and heal you from the bloody scars of destruction. That's what is important, that's the only thing that matters.

Sometimes someone around you offers nourishment for your journey and the coldness subsides for a time. Sharing your journey with another is worth it. Traveling together will shorten the loneliness and you can find laughter and contentment along the way. Pure joy and peace come at the end of your journey but you must learn to recognize these through the happiness you share with others. They will teach you a new vision. Otherwise, you will not know the ultimate sense of joy when you reach it and your journey will be longer than necessary.

CHAPTER 14

CONFRONTATION
IN A CEMETERY

This journey I was traveling through recovery included a return trip to Rebersburg and the scene of the childhood trauma. As I directed Paul to park our car near the two story, white frame house on the main street, I was surprised by the deteriorating condition of its exterior. This reality conflicted with my memory's picture of freshly painted clapboards, sturdy front porch with "gingerbread" valance around the three sides. Grandma's hand decorated rocking chair and crisp white curtains hanging inside sparkling clean windows were missing. For a few minutes, I sat on the sidewalk curb across the street. There my view was unobstructed of the first floor bay window where sunlight once had wrapped my body in warmth. Directly above on the second floor was my grandparents' bedroom window where the sunlight had been extinguished in a young child's life by a monstrous grandfather.

I remembered that the cemetery was just behind their property. I left my curbside seat, returned to Paul and the two of us walked the short distance to my grandparents' gravesite. Although no words passed between us, Paul's hand encircled mine as I approached the dead monster's burial ground. I was ready to confront Arthur Cummings and end a life of powerlessness.

I planted my feet firmly over his grave, filled my lungs with a breath of fresh country air and began, "You no longer have power over my life. I refuse to continue living behind the walls of secrecy and shame. You destroyed the innocence of a tiny child but you cannot destroy the woman I have become. You were given the responsibility of an adult grandfather but you never earned that privilege. I refuse to acknowledge you by this title. From this moment forward, you, Arthur, are to remain in limbo between heaven and hell. There you watch this woman survivor's battle for physical, emotional and spiritual victory over your crimes. Remain suspended until you learn about my courage to heal the deep wounds of incest."

As I turned away to walk the short distance to Paul's side, the afternoon sun emerged from behind a dark cloud while I heard the songs of birds accompanying our steps along the grassy path away from the graves. Now my visits to the cemetery are limited to honoring my parents, my grandmother Cummings and Aunt Thelma, the loved ones who rest in peace.

Just as much as I was able to separate my grandfather into two distinct people-the ugly monster who molested me and the gentle man who shared his love of gardening-I was able to separate myself, too.

The split: no sound of ripping pant's seams, no explosion of an atomic split, this split happened silently without fanfare. This split was as phenomenal as splitting the atom. The two-year-old child split into two distinct polarized parts. My mother defined the two, "You are such a good girl when we are with grandma and grandpa; but then when we come home, you are a bad girl."

The kewpie doll became the happy, smiling facade with angel wings and halo. She danced in the bright sunlight. The bad girl, the rebel, the seductress were all ashamed and hidden in the shadows. With an absent father and a two-faced grandfather, I realized that my first impression of men was one of confusion and fear. The uncertainty played itself out through the next fifty years of my life. I sought out positive males in the pure white light of the good girl who looked for goodness in every male while the bad girl lurked in the darkness doubting every male's intentions. Fearful of rejection and abandonment, the bad girl heeded the warning and rejected them first.

Most adults' childhood memories include stories about their best friends. I had a best friend, too. She could be trusted to keep secrets and we spent many hours together. The difference that made our friendship unique was her identity. Being an only child and an incest survivor before age two, I had some social handicaps of sorts. If a child could not trust her grandfather who could she trust? I constructed an emotional wall of protection at an early age but eventually the loneliness from inside the fortress became unbearable. Connections with others seemed impossible until an upright piano and music came along.

Church hymns, holiday carols and tunes on my radio gave a voice to pent-up feelings. Songs like *"You'll Never Walk Alone"* by Rodgers and Hammerstein, and *"Crying in the Chapel "* from 1953 were both outlets. When the piano came into my life, it offered me an outlet to pour out an emotional flood across her keyboard.

Sometimes my fingers flew furiously across her keys with an intensity that often brought Mom's remark of "hold it down in there!". Other times tears and fingertips both touched her gently while my slumped body sank deeper and deeper into the narrow bench. I have come to realize that my emotional stability during those difficult teen years was largely dependent on the piano's existence in my life.

Throughout my life, a piano followed. There was always a piece of sheet music, a book of traditional melodies or Christmas hymns tucked inside the piano bench that I could reach for when my mood needed an expression. For example, the moment that I received the dreadful telephone call at my office in the YWCA announcing my possibility of breast cancer. As soon as I could begin to absorb the frightening news; I headed for a nearby baby grand piano, sat down on the highly polished bench, touched the black and white keys and felt the comfort of a familiar friend.

CHAPTER 15

A NEW DIRECTION

B y 1989, while I continued recovery through weekly therapy, the rest of my life was shifting again. Personally, the reality of the "empty nest" phase of our life became painfully true when I noticed that my ears were still straining to hear our children's presence. My ears had been so fine tuned to locate each of our children's special sounds but now no vibrations, no echo, just silence. Then, too, the leaves of our kitchen table were no longer needed; Paul and I were face-to-face. For the first time in our life together, we were a childless couple.

Professionally, the reality of the cancer disease continued to haunt my thoughts. My ongoing question, "If I have only one year to live, how do I want to live?" eventually had an answer. I wondered if the stress of managing a multifaceted agency with government regulations, multiple supervisors, complicated sources of revenue contributed to and increased the risk of cancer returning? I didn't want to take that chance.

The months of personal experience of therapy inspired me to consider establishing my own practice. My master's degree credentials qualified me to hang a shingle outside a modest office. I was certain that self-employment would be the best chance to freedom from those many stresses of nonprofit and government agencies. I would have only myself to be answerable to for successes and failures of a private counseling practice.

With the education in accounting, experience in managing businesses, a history of self-employed Dad and Nana and a determination to launch this new venture, I set out to develop a business plan. For months, I poured over paperwork. Relinquishing the security of a $30,000 yearly salary for the uncertainty of fees for service made a three year business plan imperative. Paul's wages and health insurance benefits at his job offered us financial stability until my practice was profitable.

Once again Paul trusted my ability to launch this new venture. His abiding faith made it possible to risk yet another major decision in our life together and my career. I had a small savings to purchase the needed office equipment and supplies. The rent for a two room office in center city was manageable and I knew there were plenty of free advertising opportunities. Area women's organizations were always looking for speakers for their meetings and the topic of stress management for women was a popular subject to get an invitation to a meeting.

Also, during my position at Domestic Relations all child support checks carried my signature. That name recognition would be invaluable in establishing a business. I chose to focus my counseling practice on "Individual Counseling For Women" based on research that indicated that women are apt to seek counseling quicker than men. Research also validated that a same-sex arrangement between client and counselor increases the successful outcomes of therapy (Harriet Goldhor Learner Ph.D.)

With business plan in place, I opened the door to this new adventure, confident in success. Paul's uncertainty but abiding love boosted my faith. When day one arrived, I sat at my new desk scared that maybe I had made a terrible mistake but several weeks later the phone rang and my first client scheduled her appointment. Aided by a surge of television talk shows that focused on abuse and childhood traumas plus extended waiting lists at area counseling agencies, my business calendar was soon filled with appointments. That was twenty-two-years ago.

The combination of knowledge in psychotherapy theories and techniques along with the ability to recognize the importance of establishing a basic level of trust became the foundation of my private practice. Lincoln University, annual workshops, teachers, guides, my own recovery, clients who believed in the process of therapy and their willingness to enter into counseling with the hope of healing wounds, all combined to enhance my ability to offer them professional guidance. Each counseling session became a privilege to partner with individuals over the course of my career.

The following article hung on my office wall as a reminder of my responsibilities:

So how do you sit with a shattered soul?
Gently, with gracious and deep respect.
Patiently, for time stands still for the shattered, and the momentum of healing will be slow at first.
With the tender strength that comes from an openness to your own deepest wounding, and to your own deepest healing.
Firmly, never wavering in the utmost conviction that evil is powerful, but there is a good that is more powerful still.
Stay connected to that Goodness with all your being, however it manifests itself to you.
Acquaint yourself with the shadows that lie deep within you.
And then, open yourself, all that is you, to the Light.
Give freely. Take in abundantly.
Find your safety, your refuge, and go there as your need.

Hear what you can, and be honest about the rest: be honest at all cost.

Words won't always come; sometimes there are no words in the face of such tragic evil.

But in your willingness to be with them, they will hear you; from soul to soul they will hear that for which there are no words. Steele, K. (1987)

My personal life improved as the wounds of traumas healed and internal harmony of my distinct parts brought a wholeness. Like a breath of fresh air, I breathed without the sting of ancient fear and pain. Paul's faithful commitment to our marriage and his willingness to forgive became the foundation for building our strong loving relationship. With the safety he created through that commitment, I gradually learned the ability to give trust when another is worthy. I learned that my need for control was connected to old wounds and I was able to "let go" and love. Someone said once that "when I let go of who I am, I become who I might be."

Life holds wonderment and joy now as the pain and fear are exorcised. The awe of this healing journey through the dark deep waters continues to cleanse my soul while precious moments of joy ripple through my life and those of loved ones who choose to join the struggle and reap the harvest. Sadly, my parents chose another path, the path of denial. As I write this, I reflect on my efforts to bring them out of the darkness.

My father gave me one precious moment of himself which I will treasure. He responded lovingly when my two-year-old self told him about his father's abuse. Since then, he chose to remain in the shadow, silent and cold. I respect his choice now with some sadness for a lost father-daughter love but refuse to remain engulfed in his powerlessness and depression.

I was able to gain added knowledge into dad's lineage when my parents were preparing to move into a retirement apartment. Mom was sorting through a trunk of documents. This trunk revealed another piece of that puzzle into a family's legacy. Two newspapers from Centre County dated October 5, 1900 headlined John Cummings's suicide at age 47. My dad's grandfather had several periods of mental illness according to the article. Before hanging himself in the attic, he attempted to drink a potent mixture of a highly toxic insecticide and glass chips but neighbors prevented him from that act.

Although highly regarded by his community, the article goes on to state that "some time ago he bound two of his daughters in bed and was about to cut their throats with a razor when he was prevented from committing that awful act." This statement offered a brief insight into dad's father's possible disregard and abuse of females. It is not an excuse for this abusive behavior, but rather to understand the possible effect that his father's behavior had on his son, Arthur. The shame and embarrassment regarding 1900's concept of suicide and mental illness must have been the reason that Mom had the newspaper articles at the very bottom of that old truck. She confessed that she constantly worried that my dad would commit suicide. During the discovery of those newspapers, I was attending a family therapy training certification program. After realizing the legacy of shame that had affected at least three generations of family members, I resolved to end the chain of toxic influence. I conceived a plan to share this personal history with classmates; after all, the subject seemed relevant to our training. To my amazement, as I was making copies of the articles, waves of emotion flooded my body. Almost in rhythm with the machine's scanning, each copy brought another breaking wave. I knew immediately that a fourth generation, my own Cummings roots, had unknowingly bore the shame of a great grandfather's suicide.

My mother had repeatedly denied the reality of sexual crimes by rationalizing and minimizing every aspect of my pain. For her, the reasons were justified. I understand the after effects of her father's alcoholism, war and the era of The Great Depression on her life. I also understand fear and its impact on life's journey. I refuse to submit to these forces as Mom did. I also respect her commitment to her male God and males throughout her life, since she had been true to her own values. Those values are not mine; they belong to a generation of women who bravely weathered a different storm of survival the best way they knew. Now women claim their personal power in moving this generation through transition into an era of human equality. Our daughters will carry the torch yet another lap as they shed their mothers' survival and find their own place as another generational link in the chain.

My daughters and sons are all following their own paths. When any one shares a moment of pain or joy now I welcome the sharing, supportive and proud of their courage and growth. I know the cleansing effect of lancing deep wounds, releasing the painful poison and healing the scars of injustice, abuse and cruelty. My silent prayer to the Universe seeks justice, joy and equality for all humans whenever and wherever they may be on the road to recovery.

In my professional counseling, I am assured of the power of the human spirit to survive against all odds. Women have withstood horrible crimes and repeated daggers to their hearts and minds but the spirit lives on through the storm though *"your dreams be tossed and blown. Walk on, walk on with hope in your heart, for you'll never walk alone... you'll never walk alone.*" an inspirational line from a favorite piano piece of my past.

Both my parents died between 1996 and 2009, Dad suddenly after a heart attack, Mom gradually. Mom's health deteriorated, especially her ability to walk without frequent falls. She lived with Paul and me for several years before she moved into a nursing facility. I am grateful for those brief years with her. We became woman to woman with an acceptance of our differences. When our roles switched-she dependent; I caregiver- that transition was so much easier after our reconciliation.

Paul and I had found a new depth of a loving relationship that bloomed and blossomed after my recovery. In 2008, he was diagnosed with lung cancer. With treatments, his life remained active for three years. During that time, we fulfilled long held dreams of travel and new adventures. He suffered briefly when his tumors spread and he closed his eyes soon after. I used to tease him about that biblical phrase of marriage when two become one but now I know that half of me is missing since he is gone.

A wonderous vision appeared shortly before Paul's death. I saw myself, dressed in white, carrying him in my arms to the edge of this existence. When I was ready to hand him over to the next world, the person who was waiting to receive him was Fred. He was so grateful to Paul for loving and caring for his two children; he eagerly greeted Paul to the next phase of his journey.

Because of that vision, I dressed in white for his burial. I took comfort in knowing that the man who entered my life during a crisis, stood by my side throughout the most difficult challenges of our marriage and unselfishly loved with all his heart, was welcomed into the peace and gratitude of those in the next life.

Paul often is present to reassure me of his love and attention. Even though he is not visible, his presence is a powerful force.

I am forever grateful for all whose love in its many forms sustained me, even when I tried to push them away. I am eternally sorry for the crimes that I committed against those who were innocent victims, especially my family. From years of denial to periods of questioning, anger, depression to finally acceptance and healthy living; this journey through transitions has been both challenging and rewarding. I have learned that yesterday WAS important.

A quote from a 2009 television drama: *"Scars remind us of where we've been, they don't have to dictate where we're going."*

Note: some names have been changed as requested to protect their privacy.

ACKNOWLEDGEMENTS

During the twenty plus years of this book's development, many individuals contributed their wisdom, knowledge and assistance without hesitation whenever I sought their guidance: Penny, Susan, Mary, Pam, Betty, Judy, Jan and Rachael to mention a few. The individuals within the memoir have also contributed to my life's journey. Thanks to Friday's Writers Group for their compassion and positive feedback when I needed encouragement.

Editor Nancy Baumgartner's expertise and unending encouragement were superior. My gratitude goes beyond mere words. Margie Plotts's English Teacher skills was offered throughout the many revisions, often putting my requests before her own schedule. Thanks too for the on-call computer tech, son Greg, for his willingness to smile and always be ready to teach his computer challenged mom.

SOURCES

Bass, Ellen and Davis, Laura, 2008, *The Courage to Heal: a Guide for Women Survivors of Child Sexual Abuse*, New York, New York, HarperCollins

Courtois, Christine A., 1999, *Recollections of Sexual Abuse: Treatment Principles and Guidelines*, New York, New York, W.W. Norton & Company, Inc.

Criminal Minds; 2009, *"the slave of duty," program*

Gleen, Artie, 1953, *Crying in the Chapel, Valley Publishers*

Lamott, Anne, 1994, *Bird by Bird: Some Instructions on Writing and Life*, New York, New York, Doubleday

Lerner, Harriet Goldhor Ph.D. ,1998, *Women in Therapy*, New York, New York, Harper & Row, Publishers, Inc.

Lorde, Audrey, 1984, *Sister Outsider*, Freedom, CA, The Crossing Press

RAINN--Rape, abuse & incest. National Network website

Rodgers and Hammerstein, 1945, *Carousel, you'll never walk alone.*

Steele, K., 1987, *Sitting with the Shattered Soul*, Pilgrimage: *Journal of Personal Exploration and Psychotherapy.*

Worell, Judith and Remer, Pamela, 1996, 2003, *Feminist/Perspectives in Therapy*, Hoboken, New Jersey, John Wiley & Sons, Inc.

Bass, E. & Davis, L. (1988) (2008). *the Courage to Heal: a guide for women survivors of child sexual abuse*. New York: Harper & Row.

Blume, E.S. (1990) *Secret Survivors: Uncovering incest and its aftereffects in women*. New York: John Wiley and Sons.

Maltz, W. (1991) (2001). *the sexual healing journey: A guide for survivors of sexual abuse*. New York: HarperCollins Publishers.

National Resource Center on Domestic Violence, 800-537-2238

RAINN-Rape, Abuse & Incest Network
1220 L Street, NW Suite 505
Washington, D.C. 20005
202-544-3064 or info@rainn.org

Terr, L. (1994). *unchained memories: True stories of traumatic memories, lost and found*. New York: Harper & Row.

ABOUT THE AUTHOR

The author is currently adjusting to the lifestyle of a widow. Balancing each level of grief with the changes of living alone are the day-to-day challenges she faces. Her philosophy of approaching each new change as an opportunity to learn yet another of life's lesson has not necessarily been an opinion that she embraced as a young adult. It's been only after healing painful wounds that she was able to see through the lenses of a much healthier universe.

Now, the three aspects of her being-mind, body, spirit- each are important components in her routine self care- whether exercise and massages, ongoing knowledge opportunities, finding joy in the universe's beauty and honoring the strength of others to survive life's wounding-Rosemary's ongoing goal is celebrating life to its fullest.